What they DON'T tell you about...

WILLIAM SHAKESPEARE

Anita Ganeri

Illustrations by Alan Rowe

Consultant: James Shaw
of the Shakespeare Birthplace Trust

WAYLAND
www.waylandbooks.co.uk

Published in 2014 by Wayland

Text copyright © Anita Ganeri 2014
Illustrations © Alan Rowe 2014

Wayland
338 Euston Road
London NW1 3BH

Wayland Australia
Level 17/207 Kent Street
Sydney, NSW 2000

Cover design: Lisa Peacock
Cover illustration: Nick Hardcastle
Inside design: Diane Thistlethwaite

A CIP catalogue record for this book is available
from the British Library.
Dewey number: 822.3'3-dc23

ISBN 978 0 7502 8167 6

10 9 8 7 6 5 4 3 2 1

Printed and bound by CPI Group (UK) Ltd, Croydon, CR0 4YY

First published in 1998 by Hodder

Wayland is a division of Hachette Children's Books,
an Hachette UK Company
www.hachette.co.uk

CONTENTS

This book is for Catherine. A.G.

The quotations in this book have been taken from the **Complete Works of Shakespeare** edited by Stanley Wells and Gary Taylor.

SETTING THE SCENE

ALL THE WORLD'S A STAGE

The time: 2 p.m.
The date: Autumn, 1606
The place: The Globe Theatre, London

The theatre is hushed (well, quietish). The audience waits with bated breath (rather bad bated breath, at that). The excitement mounts. There's a flash of lightning, a crash of thunder and three hideous old witches take the stage, cackling as they go:

> 'When shall we three meet again?
> In thunder, lightning, or in rain?...'

So begins the first public performance of *Macbeth*, the latest masterpiece from the blockbusting pen of William Shakespeare. But who was this man, also known as the Bard, the Swan of Avon, or simply the greatest writer in the known world? Where did he come from and how did he do it?...

Curriculum Vitae

Name: *William Shakespeare*
(or Shaxpere, or Shagsbere etc)
Date of birth: *23 April 1564*
Place of birth: *Stratford-upon-Avon, England*
Star sign: *Taurus*
Parents: *John Shakespeare (glove-maker)
and Mary Arden (glove-maker's wife)*
Education: *Stratford Grammar School*
Marital status: *Married Anne Hathaway,
1582*
Children: *Susanna; Hamnet (not to be
confused with Hamlet) and Judith (twins)*
Occupation: *Good-ish actor; great poet;
top playwright; shrewd businessman;
glove-maker's son. Still the scourge of every
school classroom centuries after his death.*
Died: *23 April 1616, aged 52 (exactly)*

...AND WHAT DID HE LOOK LIKE?

What did Shakespeare actually look like? Reports vary. According to writer and wit, John Aubrey, who lived in the late 16th century and had never actually seen Shakespeare, he was a 'handsome, well-shaped man'. Shakespeare's good friend and fellow playwright, Ben Jonson, who had seen him close to, was not so glowing. In the foreword to Shakespeare's plays, Jonson wrote, 'Reader, look, Not on his picture, but his book'.

Was this Shakespeare?

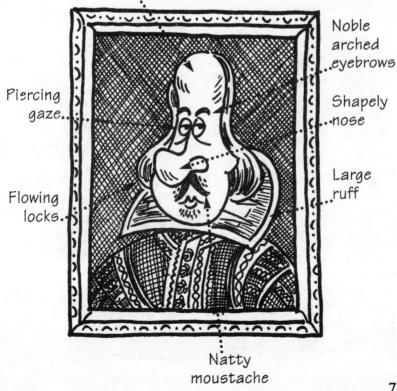

Brainy high forehead

Noble arched eyebrows

Piercing gaze

Shapely nose

Flowing locks

Large ruff

Natty moustache

7

WHAT OTHER EVIDENCE DO WE HAVE?

Not much, I'm afraid. For someone who made his living by writing, there's remarkably little (i.e. next to nothing) in the way of letters, samples of handwriting etc etc. None of the original manuscripts of Shakespeare's 37 plays, three long poems or 154 sonnets (shorter poems) have survived.

None of this seems to matter. More than 400 years after his death, the Swan of Avon is still the most acted, most performed, most printed, most reprinted, most translated writer ever. His plays are famous all over the world. There are thousands of theories, counter-theories, books and leaflets about Shakespeare. And hundreds of films, ballets, operas and musicals inspired by Shakespeare's plays (not to mention teashops, bookshops, films of the books, books of the films, T-shirts, coffee mugs etc etc...). Bardmania is big business.

But was Shakespeare in fact all he was cracked up to be? Or, in the Bard's own words, was it all really *Much Ado About Nothing?*

SHAKESPEARE'S AGE

The first thing to consider is Shakespeare's Age. Not his *actual* age, but the Age he lived in. Shakespeare's formative years were spent in the Elizabethan Age. Queen Elizabeth I came to the throne in 1558 and stayed there until 1603. These were very exciting times. The Spanish Armada was well and truly sunk. Dashingly handsome explorers, such as Raleigh and Drake, sailed to the edges of the known world and beyond. It was the Golden Age of Exploration. A big, wide world began opening up before people's eyes. They could read about it, talk about it, even put it in their pipes and smoke it - Raleigh introduced tobacco to England. And potatoes. New-fangled foreign things were all the rage. New words were needed to describe them, including the name of Shakespeare's own theatre - the Globe. Oh yes, exciting times indeed.

Of course, not everyone was happy. Mary Queen of Scots had her head cut off for being a Catholic. And, for the unfortunate Earl of Essex, it was off to lunch with the Queen one day, off with his head the next.

When Elizabeth died in 1603, James I took her place and the Jacobean Age began. James had practised ruling Scotland as James VI before travelling south to England. He should have tried harder. In 1605, a group of Gunpowder Plotters tried to blow the king to smithereens. Luckily for him, the Plot backfired and James I reigned on until 1625.

All of this had a profound effect on William Shakespeare, one way or another.

BIRTH OF THE BARD

'there was a star danced, and under that was I born.'
MUCH ADO ABOUT NOTHING

> To call him William, or not to call him William, that is the question...

William Shakespeare was most probably born in Henley Street, definitely in Stratford-upon-Avon, Warwickshire, England. Although we traditionally celebrate Shakespeare's birth on 23 April 1564, no one is sure whether this was his birthday. We know that he was baptised on 26 April, as recorded in the parish register of the Holy Trinity Church in Stratford. We also know that parents in those days usually left three days between the birth and the baptism of their children. Besides, 23 April was St George's Day - as good a date as any for a birthday. Conveniently, it also turned out to be the date that

Shakespeare died, 52 years later to the day, in 1616. (52 wasn't a bad age for the times, since many people died young of things like plague and childbirth.)

Meet the Shakespeares

William was the third child of John Shakespeare and Mary Shakespeare (or Mary Arden, as she was before she married). Two older sisters, Joan and Margaret, died before William was born. (A great many children died young in those days.) Five more children followed – three sons (Gilbert, Richard and Edmund), and two daughters (another Joan, and Anne, who died aged 8). So, William was the eldest of the family, and doubtless blamed for everything. (If you're the eldest, you'll know what I mean.)

Mr and Mrs Shakespeare

Shakespeare's mother, Mary Arden, was the favourite daughter of Richard Arden, a respectable Warwickshire gentleman. In his will, he left her some land and the goodly sum of £6 13s 6d (six pounds, thirteen shillings and sixpence – which would have been about £4,000 today.) No wonder then she was soon snapped up by young John Shakespeare, a handsome farmer's son. Some people said she'd married beneath her. After all, it was said, she could trace her ancestors back to William the Conqueror.

The Shakespeare Family Tree

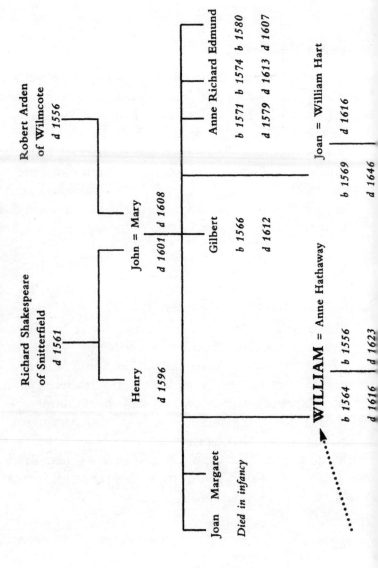

Richard Shakespeare
of Snitterfield
d 1561

Robert Arden
of Wilmcote
d 1556

John = Mary
d 1601 | *d 1608*

Henry
d 1596

Joan   Margaret
Died in infancy

WILLIAM = Anne Hathaway
b 1564 | *b 1556*
d 1616 | *d 1623*

Gilbert
b 1566
d 1612

Joan = William Hart
b 1569   *d 1616*
d 1646

Anne   Richard   Edmund
b 1571 b 1574 b 1580
d 1579 d 1613 d 1607

12

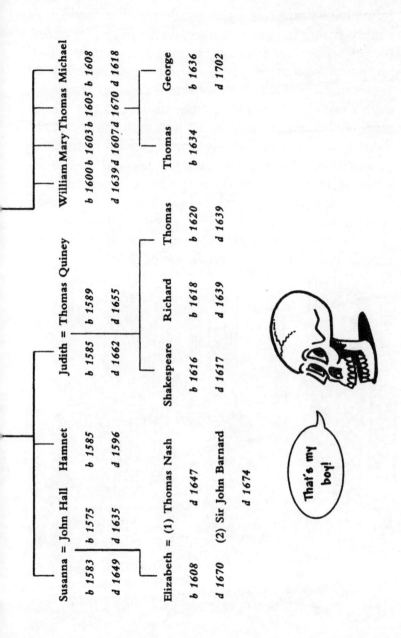

Susanna = John Hall   Hamnet   Judith = Thomas Quiney   William Mary Thomas Michael

b 1583   b 1575   b 1585   b 1585   b 1589   b 1600 b 1603 b 1605 b 1608

d 1649   d 1635   d 1596   d 1662   d 1655   d 1639 d 1607 d 1670 d 1618

Elizabeth = (1) Thomas Nash   Shakespeare   Richard   Thomas   Thomas   George

b 1608   d 1647   b 1616   b 1618   b 1620   b 1634   b 1636

d 1670   (2) Sir John Barnard   d 1617   d 1639   d 1639   d 1702

         d 1674

That's my boy!

13

John Shakespeare was a glove-maker with a mission. As a glove-maker he was in the social class of 'craftsperson', though this was a pretty respectable, highly-skilled profession which involved a long (perhaps 7-year) apprenticeship. But John Shakespeare also managed, from somewhere, to get enough money to get on the property ladder. He was soon climbing up the Stratford social scale, despite a few false starts on the way. In 1552, he was fined a shilling for making a dunghill outside his house in Henley Street. There were no dustbinmen in the Elizabethan Age and people had to leave their rubbish somewhere. But there were strict regulations about where you could leave a heap of muck and outside your front door wasn't one of them.

By 1556, a year after his marriage, John's fortunes were on the up. He became official ale and bread taster for the Borough, making sure that standards were kept up to scratch. A job not to be sniffed at.

Finally, he reached the dizzy heights of Mayor. John Shakespeare was now a top man. He wore a scarlet robe (trimmed with fur on official occasions), was guaranteed a front seat at any local events including the theatre, and owned two fine houses.

Unfortunately, in 1576, things went badly wrong. John Shakespeare ended up riddled with debt, not daring to go out in public for fear of arrest. His fall from favour probably had a number of causes - bad investments, hefty fines for money lending (which was illegal) and possible persecution for his Catholic tendencies. But as with many other aspects of Shakespeare's story, we don't know the exact details for sure. In any case, it was up to young William to save the family name ...

SHAKESPEARE'S STRATFORD

In Shakespeare's day, Stratford-upon-Avon was a small market town of 200 houses, famous for the River Avon, the Forest of Arden, lively fairs which lasted for 16 days, and leafiness (in 1582 it was recorded as having one thousand elm trees). London was just two days away by horseback; four by foot. From its place at the heart of the English countryside, Stratford was also within easy reach of the great cities of Oxford, Warwick and Worcester. A constant stream of travellers, actors, merchants and general hangers-on passed through Stratford every day. Some may have stopped to buy gloves from the Shakespeares...

THE BARD'S BIRDS

All those long walks through the Warwickshire countryside turned young William into something of a nature lover. There are over 3,000 references to birds and animals in Shakespeare's plays, not to mention the whole Forest of Arden in *As You Like It*. People used to believe that birds and animals symbolised different things. Here are some of the Bard's top birds and what they meant to him:

Cuckoo – foolish; bad singers; heralds of spring.

Magpie – bad luck.
The name magpie comes from 'maggot-pie' which meant a chattering woman, and not a rotten piece of pastry.

Cormorant – greedy and grasping.

Eagle – strong, princely and brave.

Pheasant – precious; delicious to eat.
Judges were often bribed with gifts of pheasant.

Owl – messenger of death.

Barnacle goose – a fate worse than death.
In *The Tempest*, Caliban is terrified of being turned into a barnacle goose! In Shakespeare's day, no one knew that birds migrated in winter. They thought geese suddenly appeared in spring because they miraculously hatched from tiny shellfish!

Swan – purity and virtue.

Dove – love; faithfulness; gentleness.

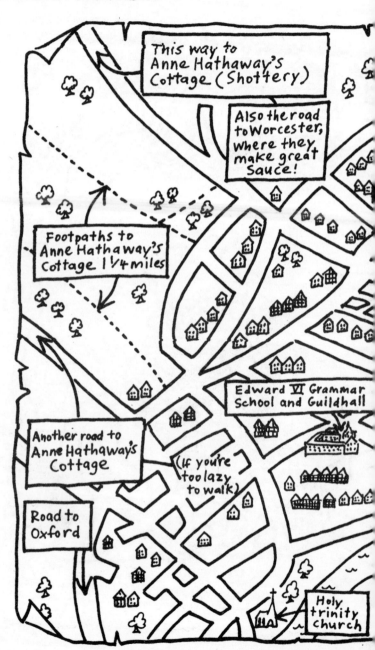

This way to Anne Hathaway's Cottage (Shottery)

Also the road to Worcester, where they make great Sauce!

Footpaths to Anne Hathaway's Cottage 1¼ miles

Edward VI Grammar School and Guildhall

Another road to Anne Hathaway's Cottage

(If you're too lazy to walk)

Road to Oxford

Holy trinity church

SHAKESPEARE'S SCHOOLDAYS

SCHOOLBOY SHAKESPEARE

Shakespeare's father was probably illiterate (could not read or write). He signed documents with his glover's mark. But when he went to 'petty school' for two years, William was taught to count, read *and* write by a master called an 'abecadarius'. He learned the alphabet and Lord's Prayer from a 'hornbook', a wooden, table-tennis-bat-shaped thing, printed on one side and blank on the other for writing practice. Then at 11, he probably began Grammar School.

SCHOOL TIMETABLE

School, in Shakespeare's day, was tough. The school day lasted from 6 or 7 o'clock in the morning to 5 or 6 o'clock at night, with two short breaks for breakfast and lunch. William's only day off was Sunday. The timetable included grammar (naturally), Latin, some Greek, classical history (i.e. Latin and Greek), poetry (mainly Latin and Greek), rhetoric (the art of speaking, much loved by Romans and Greeks), arithmetic and divinity (religious studies). A lot of the time was spent learning long passages of books by heart (yawn! yawn! yawn!).

DID SHAKESPEARE LIKE SCHOOL?

Probably not. He didn't like schoolmasters and in later life often made fun of them in his plays. More telling though is his famous description of a schoolboy from *As You Like It*:

> 'The whining schoolboy, with his satchel
> And shining morning face, creeping like snail
> Unwillingly to school.'

Is this a clue as to how Shakespeare felt? (And is this how *you* feel when you have to study Shakespeare?)

STRATFORD GRAMMAR SCHOOL
SCHOOL REPORT

Name: William Shakespeare   **Class:** 2B

Teacher: Mr Jenkins   **Age:** 12 $\frac{2}{5}$

Subject	Comments
GRAMMAR	William shows considerable promise but some of his sentences are rather long-winded.
LATIN	William seems keen on the story of Julius Caesar. This may be useful in future years.
POETRY	Excellent! Could go far.
SPEECH AND DRAMA	William tries hard but should steer clear of acting as his chosen future career.
SPELLING	Weak, but no worse than anyone else's.
CRAFTS	William's craft skills are generally poor, although he has surprised us all with his superb glove-making.

COULD SHAKESPEARE SPELL?

It depends on what you call good and bad spelling. The Elizabethans didn't go in for rules when it came to spelling. If they could write at all, they largely spelt things as they felt like it. And 's' was often written as 'f'. Filly foolf! The only actual examples of Shakespeare's own handwriting are six versions of his signature, all spelt differently. In fact, over 80 different versions are known altogether. So Shakespeare was also known as:

Shagsper

Shaxpere

Shackespere

Shakeshaft

Shapeare

to name but a few.

All the signatures have one thing in common. For the greatest playwright ever known, Shakespeare had terrible handwriting – spidery, scrawly and jerky. Of course, he did have to write with a quill pen (biros had not been invented). And he'd already done so much writing that he probably suffered from writer's cramp.

TRAVELLING PLAYERS

Every so often, companies of travelling actors arrived in town, ready to perform the latest plays. Plays and actors were incredibly popular. In one place, the crowd smashed the town hall windows to get a sneak preview of the stars.

In 1569, the Queen's Men played at the Guildhall in Stratford. It was lucky for William that his father was Mayor - the Shakespeares had the best seats in the house. The actors were paid 9 shillings for their work. Though only five at the time, it wasn't long before William was well and truly bitten by the acting bug.

In 1587, another (different) company of the same name reached the town. They'd suffered a terrible blow. One of their leading actors, William Knell, had been stabbed and killed, and someone was needed to take his place. That someone *may* have been Shakespeare. But once again, we don't know for certain, as the whole story is shrouded in mystery. It may never have happened, or it may even have been invented by scholars as a convenient way of tying up some loose ends and pushing Shakespeare into acting! We'll never know for sure...

THE SCHOOL OF LIFE

Meanwhile John Shakespeare's troubles seem to have put an early end to Shakespeare's schooldays. Instead of going to university, he went to work for his father where his glove-making skills came in very handy.

LOVE AND MARRIAGE

HAVE YOU WASHED MY RUFF, ANNE?

Glove-making was not all that William got up to. On 27 November 1582, after a whirlwind romance, he married Anne Hathaway. He was 17. She was 26 - and three months pregnant! A special marriage licence was issued so that William and Anne could tie the knot at the local parish church.

The Shakespeares and Hathaways were not best pleased. They probably felt cheated, too, because in those days, people liked to have a small bet on whether the bride would say 'Yes'! (They also bet on dogs.) Girls and their mothers had a wide choice of books full of top tips on how to catch a husband.

Victorian scholars were embarrassed by the thought of Shakespeare being involved in a scandal. So they came up with the idea of a 'pre-marriage contract', an arrangement which made everything nice and respectable again. There was really no such thing, at least not in Shakespeare's case.

WHO WAS ANNE HATHAWAY?

Good question. Anne was the daughter of Richard Hathaway, a farmer from Shottery near Stratford. She stayed in Stratford while William made his name in London and so she probably never even got to see a Shakespeare play!

The best that can be said of Anne Hathaway is that she was very ordinary. Some people say Anne tricked William into marriage. After all, she was 26 – which people then considered to be a bit past it in marriage terms! Strangely, the name on the special marriage licence is not Anne Hathaway of Shottery, but Anne Whateley of Temple Grafton. So, who *did* Shakespeare marry? The usual explanation is that the clerk's pen slipped as he filled in the register. He'd written Whateley in an earlier entry and the name had stuck in his mind. Another rumour is that Anne W was William's true love but he was forced to marry Anne H instead (see above).

'But love is blind, and lovers cannot see
The pretty follies that themselves commit.'
MERCHANT OF VENICE

DADDY!

William and Anne's first child, Susanna, was born six months after their wedding and baptised on 26 May 1583. Two years later, two more little Shakespeares arrived, the twins, Hamnet (yes, Ham*n*et) and Judith. They were named after Hamnet and Judith Sadler, the Shakespeares' best friends and the twins' godparents. (The Sadlers later returned the favour by naming their son William.)

THE LOST YEARS – WHERE DID THEY GO?

So far so good. In 1585, we know that Shakespeare was living happily in Stratford with his wife, daughter and new-born twins. But then what? From 1585-1591, the trail goes cold. We have absolutely no records whatsoever about where Shakespeare was during that time or what he was up to. These are Shakepeare's famous 'lost years'.

How did Shakespeare manage to lose them? To lose one year seems unlucky. To lose seven seems extremely careless. There are plenty of theories about what happened during the lost years, though not a shred of evidence to back them up. Look at the options:

Did Shakespeare join his father as an apprentice glove-maker?

Did he work for a local butcher?

Did he sail to Italy?
He often mentions Italy in his plays.

Did he study the law?
He uses many legal terms in his plays.

Was he forced to leave Stratford in disgrace? The story goes that he was caught poaching deer.

Did he teach at the local grammar school? This is the theory put forward by John Aubrey. But would you trust a man described by his friends as 'shiftless...roving and maggoty'!

Did he join the travelling players when they visited Stratford?

Did he run off to London to seek fame and fortune? Legend has it that he got a job as a horse-holder at the theatre doors, guarding people's horses while they watched the plays.

Did he learn Spanish and join the Armada?

Or did he enlist in the English army to fight the Spanish?

Who knows?

Or none of the above?

What we do know for certain is that by 1592, Shakespeare was in London, busy making a name for himself as an actor and playwright.

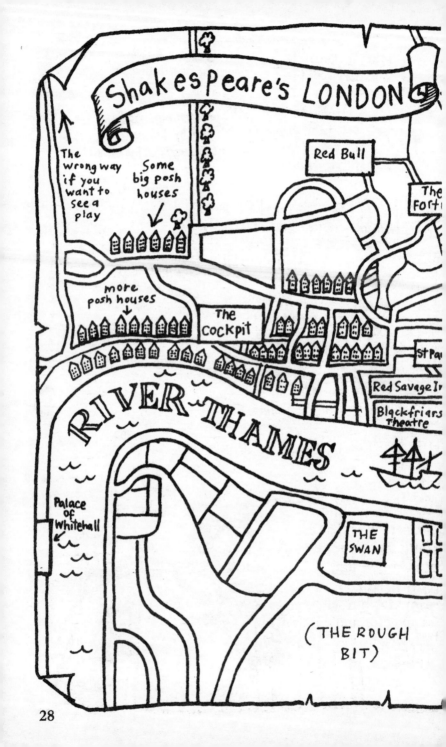

Shakespeare's LONDON

The wrong way if you want to see a play

Some big posh houses

Red Bull

The Fort...

more posh houses

The Cockpit

St Pau...

Red Savage In...

Blackfriars Theatre

RIVER THAMES

Palace of Whitehall

THE SWAN

(THE ROUGH BIT)

To somewhere
North of
London.
(Maybe Watford)

N
W E
S

The
Theatre

The
Curtain

Bull Inn

Boar's
Head Inn

Cross keys
Inn

Red Lion
Playhouse

Bell Inn

THE TOWER

The Theatre
not the flower

LONDON
BRIDGE
Cross here
to get
mugged.

(Hostel for the
headless)

THE CLINK

THE
LOBE

good place
to see
a play

(THE
EVEN
ROUGHER
BIT)

SHAKESPEARE IN LONDON

CITY LIFE

London must have been a shock to a country boy. At this time, it was a huge, thriving city of about 200,000 people. Dirty, smelly, overcrowded and not terribly safe, it was still an exciting place to live in.

Queen Elizabeth I ruled from the Palace of Whitehall and woe betide anyone who forgot it. The heads of executed traitors were displayed on spikes at the city gates to show who was boss.

As Shakespeare walked to work, he might have paused for thought outside London's notorious prisons – Newgate, the Marshalsea, the Fleet, the Clink and the Tower of London itself. He almost certainly browsed among the bookstalls in the yard outside St Paul's Cathedral. Travel books were big business, with the current boom in exploration and adventuring.

The south bank show

The most dangerous, most unsavoury part of London lay to the south of the River Thames. This was the notorious Bankside in Southwark, infamous for gambling, drinking, petty crime and low life. Bankside had inns, brothels, bear-baiting pits and many other undesirable places of entertainment, including theatres. It lay outside the City walls, and, more importantly, outside the reach of the City authorities, who kept an eye on public morals. In Bankside, anything went... and frequently did.

Crossing the river

For Elizabethans out for a good time, there was only one way to get to Bankside - across the River Thames. Many people travelled across in small ferries, called 'wherries'. You knew which way the wherries were going by the ferrymen's (wherrymen's?) cries of 'Westward Ho!' or 'Eastward Ho!'. The ferrymen were a powerful lot. When they heard of a plan to move the theatres across the river to the north bank, they put a stop to it. It would have been very bad for business. Things were hard enough when the theatres were closed by plague or the river froze over in winter.

Alternatively, you could save the ferry fare and walk across London Bridge. The only bridge across the river, it had 15 arches and was lined with cramped rows of dingy shops and houses. At either end, more traitors' heads were stuck on poles. Some people said that the Queen couldn't have been very popular if there were so many traitors (but they said it very quietly).

Rented rooms

In London, Shakespeare rented a room, first in Bishopsgate, an area popular with actors and famous for its local lunatic asylum, known as Bedlam. On Sundays, Londoners flocked the Bedlam to stare at the unfortunate inmates! Next Shakespeare moved south to Bankside, to be closer to the theatres. Or so he said. He was also in trouble with the Bishopsgate authorities for not paying his taxes (a small matter of 13 shillings and 4 pence – about £400 in today's money). They finally caught up with him and he paid up. Otherwise he might have ended up in Clink himself!

In 1599, he left Bankside and moved in with the Mountjoys of Silver Street, Cripplegate. Christopher Mountjoy made fancy wigs and ladies' hats. Not ordinary fancy wigs, of course. One cost £50 – about £29,500 at today's prices!

Having a good time, the Elizabethan way

Elizabethans loved a good day out. The bloodier, the better. They flocked to public executions, fighting to get ringside seats. Condemned men were expected to put on a show for the crowds, with dramatic final speeches from the scaffold. By contrast, the Sunday sermons at St Paul's also drew large crowds.

A BIT OF BEAR-BAITING

The grisly spectacle of bear-baiting was hugely popular. People flocked to the Bear Garden in Bankside to watch bears, and bulls, chained to stakes, being set on by very large, very hungry dogs. Bets were laid on which would last longest. The crowd roared and cheered as the animals tore into

each other. Star bears, such as George Stone and Harry Hunks, became household names. So important was bear-baiting that the Keeper of the Bears was appointed by the Queen herself.

I WAS THERE - AN EYEWITNESS ACCOUNT

'There is a round building three stories high, in which are kept about a hundred large English dogs, with separate wooden kennels for each of them. These dogs were made to fight singly with three bears, the second bear being larger than the first and the third larger than the second. After this, a bull was brought in and chased by the dogs, and at last a bull, who defended himself most bravely.'

Lupold Von Wedel, visitor to Southwark, 1584

CRAZY FOR THE THEATRE

And if bear-baiting, bull-baiting, cock-fighting, sermons and beheadings weren't enough, there was always the theatre. Londoners were crazy about the theatre, flocking to see the latest plays and ogle at their favourite actors. Anyone could go to the theatre, and anyone did. Today, you'd take out a video. In the Elizabethan Age, you'd have gone to the theatre.

A German visitor to London wrote that, *'Daily, at two in the afternoon, London has two, sometimes three plays running in different places, competing with each other, and those which play best obtain most spectators'*. About 21,000 stage-struck Londoners went to the theatre every week, on every day except Sunday. That's over a tenth of the city's entire population. People were as keen on the theatre then, as we are on football today.

Down with fun!

The theatre was not to everyone's taste. The Puritans (party-poopers all) and the City authorities (no fun at all) utterly disapproved. Here's what they thought:

1. That the theatres kept people off work (plays were performed in the afternoons).

2. That they were unhealthy, germ-ridden flea pits.

In Shakespeare's day, there were frequent outbreaks of plague. If more than 30-40 people died in a week, the City authorities closed the theatres, usually for a few days at a time. In 1592-93, 1603 and 1609, the plague hit epidemic proportions. The theatres were closed for months on end and the actors forced to go on tour. They were not allowed back to London until the plague had died down.

Plague facts

✖ The plague was spread by blood-sucking fleas which lived on black rats.

✖ Some 50,000 people died in the plagues of 1592-93, 1603 and 1609.

✖ Symptoms included:
  • boils in the armpits and groin
  • red rashes all over the body
  • high fever
  • vomiting
  • agonising pain
  • death (usually within 3 days)

✖ There was no known cure.

* People thought God had sent the plague to punish them for their wickedness.

* Plague doctors wore special masks with 'beaks' filled with spices. These were thought to protect them from infection.

* People stuffed rosemary in their ears and noses for protection.

* Plague victims' houses were boarded up and large, red crosses painted on their doors.

3. The Puritans also believed that the theatres encouraged crime and vice. (It's true they were a pickpocket's paradise.)

4. They also thought that the plays set a bad example for people to copy.

Matters came to such a head that, on 13 September 1595, the Lord Mayor of London wrote to the Privy Council:

> 'We have been told heretofore to signify to you: the great inconvenience that groweth to this City by the common exercise of stage plays ... containing nothing but profane fables, lascivious matters, cozening devices, and other unseemly and scurrilous behaviours ...'

In other words, the Puritans didn't like the theatre!

A TRIP TO THE THEATRE

In Shakespeare's day, performances began at 2 o'clock sharp. (The actors spent the morning rehearsing.) Posters and handbills advertised the play. A silk flag fluttered from the theatre roof signalling that there would be a performance today. And just before the play began, a trumpet sounded from the tower to hurry people along. There were performances every day except Sunday and during Lent (though this rule was often ignored). From October to April, the theatre closed because it wasn't protected from the weather. As it was, rain sometimes stopped play.

WHO WENT TO THE THEATRE?

Anyone and everyone went to the theatre. It didn't matter who you were - a servant, a student or a duke with a free afternoon. The better off you were, the better your seat. Ticket prices ranged from a penny for standing room in the yard around the stage (this section of the audience was called groundlings), to twopence for a seat in the lower gallery (a cushion cost a penny extra), up to sixpence for the upper gallery or a seat on the stage, and a shilling for a private 'gentlemen's room' or box. It can't have been much fun being a groundling watching *Hamlet*. The play lasted for hours! For the upper classes, the theatre gave them the chance to show off new clothes and catch up on the latest scandal and gossip.

> A penny for a ticket was a bargain in those days. Tobacco cost three pence a pipeful. A bag of nuts cost sixpence.

Box-office business

A group of 'gatherers' (usually actors) stood at the theatre doors and collected the ticket money. This was locked in a box until the performance was over. (Then it was divided among the sharers.) This is how we got the term 'box-office' which is still used today.

There was no way of reserving seats. You had to get there early. Some people arrived a good hour or so before the play began.

Audience participation

Unlike a modern audience, Elizabethan theatre-goers saw no reason to keep quiet during a play.
They shuffled their feet, whistled, clapped, cheered, picked their noses and picked pockets. They booed loudly and heckled if they didn't like what they saw, and sang along to any songs.

Hiss...

Boo!

Have a tast orange

Get off yer rubbish!

They roared with laughter at the jokes and wept buckets at the sad bits. They ate and drank throughout the play. There were always bottles of beer, nuts and fruit on sale. If the play was bad, they threw handfuls of peel at the actors. Some actors complained. It wasn't easy to say your lines when all around you were the sounds of nuts being cracked and beer being guzzled.

With all that eating and drinking, and the strong whiff of garlic (used to ward off evil spirits), things got very smelly down in the yard. The toilets, if any, were open buckets, which didn't help improve things at all!

Special effects

There weren't many props or special effects. People went to the theatre to *hear* a play, rather than see a grand spectacle. The stage was bare for much of the action, with perhaps a small shrub to suggest a forest. Some special effects came from the 'Heavens' (above the stage). Here cannonballs were rolled around to sound like thunder and fireworks set off to suggest lightning.

Actors on thrones or in chariots were winched down on to the stage. The trapdoor, leading into 'Hell', was used to show a grave or a dungeon. Other props included bladders filled with pigs' blood and worn under costumes for stabbing scenes. Night scenes were shown by lighted candles.

There is an inventory for the Rose Theatre which reads something like this:

PHILIP HENSLOWE'S INVENTORY OF PROPS FROM THE ROSE THEATRE:

ITEM: 1 rock, 1 cage, 1 tomb, 1 Mouth of Hell

ITEM: 2 steeples, 1 chime of bells, 1 beacon

ITEM: 1 globe, 1 golden sceptre, 3 clubs

ITEM: the city of Rome

ITEM: 1 golden fleece, 2 rackets, 1 bay tree

ITEM: 1 wooden canopy

ITEM: 8 masks

ITEM: Cupid's bow and arrows, a cloth showing the sun and the moon

ITEM: 2 mossy banks, 1 snake

Dressing the Part

Costumes were a different story. They mattered very much indeed and were often lavish and colourful. From a character's costume, the audience could tell their social status as well as their personality. Sometimes noblemen left fine clothes to their servants when they died. The servants couldn't wear them so they sold them to acting companies instead. Costumes were a company's most treasured possessions. Edward Alleyn once paid £20 for a black velvet gown – a third of what Shakespeare paid for a fine house in Stratford. Actors were fined more for stealing a costume than for missing a performance!

A law in 1597 banned the lower classes from wearing fine or fancy clothes. From now on, fashion was strictly for the rich and famous. Silks, velvets, ruffs (the bigger, the better) and hooped petticoats were all the rage.

The Elizabethans had only a vague idea about how people dressed in the past. So, for plays set in Rome (e.g. *Titus Andronicus* or *Julius Caesar*), the actors mostly wore Elizabethan clothes, with the odd toga thrown in!

Fines

Actors were fined for breaking the rules. The system of fines was written into their contracts.

For arriving late at rehearsals	12 pence
For missing rehearsals altogether	2 shillings
For not being ready for a performance	3 shillings
For being drunk on stage	10 shillings
For missing a performance	20 shillings
For stealing costumes	40 pounds

FIRST THEATRES

Before 1576, the Red Lion Playhouse, London, was the only purpose-built theatre, so actors performed wherever they could – in innyards, country houses, university colleges and, if they were in favour, at court.

When it came to theatres proper, these had to be built outside the City walls as theatre-going was frowned on by the authorities. The first such theatre, called The Theatre (obviously) was built in Shoreditch (east London) in 1576. Another theatre, called The Curtain appeared soon after.

By 1587, the theatre scene had shifted to Bankside. If a play was rubbish, you could always catch a bout of bear-baiting or drown your sorrows at the nearest inn. Between 1587-1599, three new theatres – the Rose, the Swan and the Globe – were built in Bankside. The Bear Garden itself was converted into the Hope Theatre in 1614.

THE ROSE

The Rose was the first theatre built in Bankside, in 1587. It was owned by the great theatrical entrepreneur, Philip Henslowe and was home to the Lord Admiral's

Men, a company led by the most famous actor of his day, Edward Alleyn. The Rose closed down in 1602, unable to compete with Shakespeare's Globe.

The Swan

The Swan opened its doors in 1596. A Dutch visitor, Johannes de Witt, had this to say about it:

> 'Of all the theatres, however, the largest and most magnificent is that whose sign is a swan, for it will seat 3,000 people, is built of flint stones ... and is supported by wooden columns so painted as to deceive the sharpest observer into thinking they are marble...'

But the Swan was also jinxed. In 1597, a play was put on which the authorities thought so offensive they ordered the Swan and all the other theatres to be closed.

The Globe

In 1599, Shakespeare and the Lord Chamberlain's Men (see page 55) took up residence in a new theatre on Bankside, called the Globe. It wasn't *brand* new, strictly speaking, but was built from the timbers of the old Theatre in Shoreditch after an argument about the lease. In the dead of night, the Theatre was dismantled, beam by beam, by a carpenter called Peter Street and twelve helpers (including actors). It was ferried secretly across the river and rebuilt on the Bankside. The wood might be recycled but the name was new – a new word for a new world opened up by the Elizabethan explorers. Soon it was on everyone's lips.

One of the first plays performed at the Globe was Shakespeare's *Henry V* (in the prologue of which the theatre is described as a wooden 'O'). Over the next 14 years, the theatre flourished and Shakespeare appeared regularly in his own and Ben Jonson's plays. Then, on 29 June 1613, disaster struck. During the first performance of Shakespeare's *Henry VIII* a cannon backfired, setting fire to the thatched roof. In two hours flat, the whole theatre had burned down. Amazingly, no one was hurt apart from one man whose trousers caught fire. He put the flames out with the mugful of beer! An eyewitness, Sir Henry Wotton, described the scene in a letter:

'Only one man had his breeches set on fire, that would perhaps have broiled him, if he had not by the benefit of a provident wit put it out with bottle-ale.'

Within a year, the Globe was rebuilt and back in business. It had a tiled roof this time, for safety. In 1642, the theatre was closed down by the Puritans and, two years later, completely demolished. A block of tenements (flats) was built in its place.

What did the Globe look like?

No pictures of the Globe survive but we've a good idea of what it looked like. It was a half-timbered, five-sided building (rather than a perfect O), with a thatched roof above the galleries. The yard was open to the sky. It could hold a full house of some 2,500 people.

THE GLOBE
(Side view)

Thatched roof over galleries.

A flag flying above the theatre advertised performances. The Globe's emblem was the god, Hercules, carrying the world on his shoulders.

Winch tower
Containing machinery for lowering actors on to the stage.

Walls
Covered in lime plaster.

Creaky stairs

Stage roof
Thatched roof above the stage.

Heavens The underside of the stage roof, painted sky-blue and decorated with stars, moons and suns.

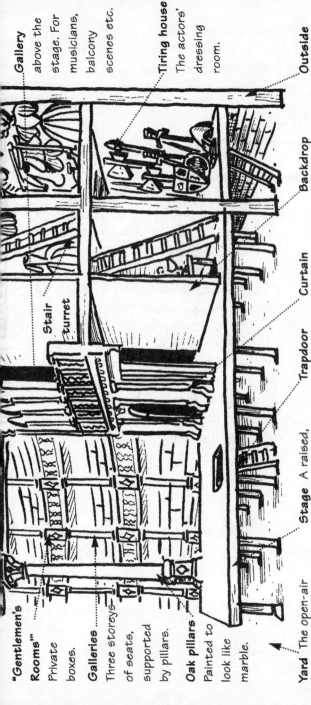

Gallery above the stage. For musicians, balcony scenes etc.

Tiring house The actors' dressing room.

Outside walls About 12 metres high.

Backdrop A curtain, usually painted with trees, flowers etc.

Curtain Separating the stage from the backstage area.

Trapdoor Leading down into Hell, the space under the stage.

Stair turret

"Gentlemen's Rooms" Private boxes.

Galleries Three storeys of seats, supported by pillars.

Oak pillars Painted to look like marble.

Stage A raised, rectangular stage, sticking out into the yard. It only had space for 12 actors, at most, to appear at a time.

Yard The open-air standing room in front of the stage. The floor was covered with hard-wearing earth, ash and hazelnut shells.

45

THE HOPE

In 1614, Henslowe bought the Bear Garden and converted it into a theatre. The Hope Theatre had a moveable stage to allow for plays on four days a week and bear-baiting on the other two. It was finally demolished in 1656.

BLACKFRIARS

Elizabethan theatres were open to the elements, fine in summer but not so great in winter. But in 1609, Shakespeare's company took over Blackfriars, an indoor hall built on the ruins of a Catholic monastery, as their winter headquarters. (Blackfriars was also the scene of the trial of Catherine of Aragon, first wife of Henry VIII, Elizabeth I's larger-than-life father.) Blackfriars was an indoor, artificially lit, all-seater theatre (unlike the Globe). These new developments not only made the experience of theatre-going much more like it is today, but also opened up new theatrical possibilities for Shakespeare, which are partly responsible for the developing style of his later plays. Theatre-going at Blackfriars was also responsible for some of the earliest recorded traffic jams! The building was pulled down in 1655.

AN ACTOR'S LIFE

ACTING THE PART

Life as an Elizabethan actor meant long hours and extremely hard work. With a huge turnover of plays, there were hundreds of lines to learn - probably around 800 a day! Actors rarely had the luxury of playing the same part two days in a row. They often had to double up in parts and help with props, costumes, directing, prompting, set design, special effects (fireworks, music etc) and with selling tickets and refreshments. By the time of the performance itself, they were probably completely exhausted!

Many actors began their professional lives young, playing in children's companies. Others joined adult companies at the age of 10-13 years old. Some were apprenticed to the company's more senior actors. That way they could learn on the job.

Things were not always as they seemed. Women were not allowed to act, so boys played female parts instead (until their voices broke). All of Shakespeare's greatest leading ladies - Lady Macbeth, Juliet and Cleopatra - were originally played by men.

There's Cleo!

Isn't he gorgeous!

Sometimes, boys played women dressed up as men, for example, the actor playing Rosalind disguised as Ganymede in *As You Like It*. It could all get very complicated indeed.

For actors who made it, great things lay in store. They were treated as superstars, with their own fan clubs and groupies. When the Queen's Men were touring in 1587, the actors were mobbed wherever they went.

WERE YOU BORN FOR THE STAGE?

Do *you* have what it took to be an Elizabethan actor? Could *you* have been a Tudor superstar? Answer yes or no to the following questions:

1	*Are you a boy?*	Yes	No
2	*Can you learn lines?*	Yes	No
3	*Are you good with your hands?*	Yes	No
4	*Are you sporty (fencing's a must)?*	Yes	No
5	*Can you play a musical instrument?*	Yes	No
6	*Do you look good in a dress?*	Yes	No
7	*Can you sing and dance?*	Yes	No
8	*Is your speaking voice clear and strong?*	Yes	No
9	*Have you got stamina? (You'll need it!)*	Yes	No
10	*Are you prepared to start at the bottom?*	Yes	No
11	*Can you cope with the pressures of fame?*	Yes	No

How did you score?

8-10 yeses: *Bravo! Shakespeare would have been proud of you!*

5-7 yeses: *Not bad! The actor's life may well be for you but you'll need to concentrate harder at rehearsals.*

4 and below: *Forget it! Perhaps glove-making might be more up your street!*

TREADING THE BOARDS

The first mention of Shakespeare the actor is not very flattering. In an article called *Greene's Groatsworth of Wit Bought with a Million of Repentance*, fellow writer, Robert Greene, describes him as an 'upstart crow', and an 'absolute Jack-of-all-trades'. Shakespeare himself seemed content to play minor roles, such as the ghost in *Hamlet* and Adam, the servant, in *As You Like It*. He was also known to act in plays by other writers, such as his friend, Ben Jonson.

Perhaps it was sour grapes on Greene's part. He was, as it were, green with envy at Shakespeare's writing talents. To be outdone by a man from the country, who had no education to speak of, was more than he could bear. In fact, his attack on Shakespeare became his greatest claim to fame. He died in 1592, after stuffing himself stupid on pickled herrings and red wine.

Everyone else commented on Shakespeare's good manners and gentle nature. By 1592, he was listed as an actor with the Lord Chamberlain's Men. In the same year, his first play, *Henry VI Part 1*, was performed. It was a huge hit. The world, it seemed, was quickly becoming Shakespeare's oyster.

The Lord Chamberlain's Men

Each theatre had its own actors. Shakespeare joined the Lord Chamberlain's Men, playing at the Globe (in summer) and later at Blackfriars (in winter). Other famous members of this company were Richard Burbage and Will Kempe. Shakespeare was chief playwright, with a ready market for his work. He also acted and directed. He matched the parts he wrote to the actors' talents. The meatiest roles (Romeo, Hamlet, Macbeth, Lear etc) went to Burbage, who specialised in tragedy. Kempe played the fool (until, rumour has it, he got on Shakespeare's nerves and left the company).

The company had its other colourful characters. Another clown, Thomas Pope, took a housekeeper called Goodwife Willingson and adopted children as a hobby. John Heminges, the company's accountant, had 12 children of his own. Augustine Phillips only had five, but owned a large collection of musical instruments.

In 1603, Shakespeare's company received their highest honour. By royal appointment to James I, they became the King's Men.

Keeping company

The Lord Chamberlain's Men was not the only acting company making a name for itself. Its rivals were hot on its heels. In the 1580s, the leading actors were the Queen's Men, selected by Her Majesty herself. Their star was the clown, Richard Tarlton, who was also the Queen's private jester.

LORD ADMIRAL'S MEN

Founded in 1594, the Lord Admiral's Men performed at various theatres run by Philip Henslowe, money-lender and theatre manager extraordinaire (thanks to a wealthy wife and a nose for business). From 1592, Henslowe kept a diary giving dates of new plays and box-office takings, plus the odd card trick, recipe and spell, such as one 'to make a fowl fall dead'. (A diary meant a notebook in those days.) Henslowe was not an easy man to work for. He paid just £6 for a new play, often in £1 instalments. His star player was the great Edward Alleyn, who also happened to be his son-in-law. The famous diary passed to him when Henslowe died.

CHILDREN'S COMPANIES

Shakespeare's greatest rivals were not, however, the Queen's Men nor even Henslowe's lot. They were children's companies, made up entirely of choir boys from the Chapel Royal and St Paul's Cathedral. They sang, danced and looked sweet and, rather sickeningly for Shakespeare, everyone thought they were wonderful.

If it wasn't for you meddling, pesky kids...!

FAMOUS ACTORS OF SHAKESPEARE'S DAY

And the winners are . . .

1. RICHARD BURBAG

Born: 1567   **Died:** 1619

Company: Lord Chamberlain's Men/King's Men

Famous roles: Tragic heroes (Hamlet, Lear, Macbeth etc)

Claim to fame: The greatest tragic actor of his day. Founder member of the Lord Chamberlain's Men and a talented painter (he may have painted Shakespeare's portrait). Famous for his chestnut locks and fiery temper.

2. EDWARD ALLEYN

Born: 1566   **Died:** 1626

Company: Lord Admiral's Men

Famous roles: Tragic heroes (e.g. Tamburlaine, the Jew of Malta and Doctor Faustus)

Claim to fame: Burbage's arch rival. Philip Henslowe's son-in-law and co-owner of the Rose and Fortune theatres. Founder of Dulwich College (a famous London public school). Famous for his loud voice and many farewell performances. In a letter to his wife, he called her his 'good, sweet mouse' and asked her to dye his orange stockings black.

3. RICHARD TARLTON

Died: 1588

Company: The Queen's Men
Famous roles: Fools and clowns.
Claim to fame: The greatest comic actor of his day and Elizabeth I's court jester. Famous for inventing jigs (comic dances) and for pulling funny faces. Tarlton fell out of favour with the Queen for daring to criticise Walter Raleigh. He then ran an inn in London. His trademark was his russet-coloured suit, buttoned cap and drum which had audiences rolling in the aisles.

4. WILLIAM KEMPE

Career: 1585-1603
Company: Lord Chamberlain's Men
Famous roles: Clowns and fools (e.g. Peter in Romeo and Juliet; Dogberry in Much Ado About Nothing)
Claim to fame: The other greatest comic actor of his day, particularly good at slapstick. Founder-member of the Lord Chamberlain's Men. Kempe got on Shakespeare's nerves for laughing at his own jokes. He left the company in 1599 to morris-dance from London to Norwich. It took nine days and was a great success!

KNOWING YOUR PLACE

Each company had a strict pecking order. At the bottom of the pile came the boy apprentices, the company dogs' bodies. If they were good enough, they could work their way up to the rank of 'hired men', employed as extras and backstage staff. (This is probably where Shakespeare started.) At the top were the 'sharers', leading actors who owned shares in the company and theatre. They also trained apprentices (Shakespeare seems to have escaped this extra duty). In a company such as the Lord Chamberlain's Men, there were 2–4 boy apprentices, 5–6 hired men and 8–9 sharers.

A SHARE OF THE PROFITS

Shakespeare paid about £30 for his shares in the Lord Chamberlain's Men (around £18,000 in today's money), and a further £100 (worth approximately £60,000 now) for a tenth share in the new Globe Theatre. In return, he got a cut of the profits. The shareholders divided half the profits between them and ploughed the other half back into the theatre. As London's leading playwright, Shakespeare did very nicely out of it all. With his other business interests in Stratford (he invested in land and property there) he was soon a wealthy man, raking in about £250 a year (which would be around £148,000 now).

are a penny for sturdy Beggar

VAGRANTS AND VAGABONDS

The government was nervous. There were too many travelling players roaming the country, causing mischief and mayhem. In 1572, they passed the Vagabonds Act. From now on, all jugglers, tinkers, pedlars, bear-keepers and common players were known as 'sturdy beggars'. Unless they had an employer, and a licence to prove it, they were classed as vagabonds and punished accordingly.

To get a licence, actors needed someone to back their company and give it a name. Someone wealthy and powerful. The search for a sponsor was on...

WHO BACKED SHAKESPEARE?

Shakespeare had friends in high places. Before he joined them, the Lord Chamberlain's Men were called Strange's Men after their sponsor, Ferdinando, Lord Strange, Earl of Derby. Strange rumours surrounded Lord Strange's death. He'd been bewitched, they said. And, despite being dosed with best rhinoceros horn, he died in 1594, aged 35. The company then came under the Lord Chamberlain's care, and later, the patronage of King James himself.

Shakespeare also had a personal sponsor - Henry Wriothesley (pronounced Rizzly), Earl of Southampton. To butter him up, Shakespeare dedicated two poems, *Venus and Adonis*, and *The Rape of Lucrece*, to him. The ploy worked and Shakespeare was rewarded in cash. By all accounts, Southampton was dashing and handsome, and a bit of a twit, with a fancy taste in clothes. But he knew a good poem when he saw one.

WRITING PLAYS AND PLAYWRIGHTING

Acting, directing, shareholding and writing plays kept Shakespeare busy. His skills were much in demand. Audiences wanted new plays and they wanted them fast.

The theatres put on six plays a week, six days a week, with about 30 plays a season (from autumn to early summer), half of them new. In 1594-95, the Lord Admiral's Men performed 38 plays, 21 of which were new. It was very demanding on all concerned. Shakespeare kept up a steady stream of work, writing on average two new plays a season.

Of course, Shakespeare was lucky (as well as being enormously talented). He had a ready market for his plays and they were huge box-office hits. Other playwrights were not so fortunate. Many ended up in debtors' prisons, literally 'in the Clink'. In his diary, Henslowe notes his takings from plays performed at the Rose Theatre. A run of Shakespeare's *Henry VI Part 1* earned him £3 16s 8d (about £2,200 in today's money) whereas Robert Greene's *Friar Bacon* and *Friar Bungay* took just 17s 3d. (approximately £500). No wonder Greene hated Shakespeare so much.

FELLOW PLAYWRIGHTS, OR THE COMPETITION!

Being a playwright in Elizabethan times was not without its dangers. Playwrights often lived in seedy parts of London where they rubbed shoulders with petty crooks, conmen, thieves and the like. Somehow Shakespeare steered clear of trouble. Others walked straight into it. Remember poor old Robert Greene? The only person at his deathbed was his ex-mistress, the seedy sister of a highwayman, called Cutting Jack Ball. (He was later hanged.)

When shall we two - no, no - three ...

MARLOWE'S LAST STAND

R.I.P.

Name: CHRISTOPHER MARLOWE

Born: 6 February 1564 **Died:** 30 May 1593

Greatest works: *Tamburlaine; The Jew of Malta; Doctor Faustus*

Life and times: Marlowe often got into trouble with the authorities for his anti-Church writings (you could be burnt at the stake for less). But before he could be brought to trial, he was stabbed through the eye in a tavern brawl, apparently in an argument over the bill.

The man who killed Marlowe was never caught. It's possible that Marlowe's friend, Sir Thomas Walsingham, had Marlowe murdered to save his own skin. Or that Sir Thomas pretended to have him killed and in fact had spirited him away to begin a new life somewhere else.

As far as Shakespeare was concerned, all this was good news. A serious rival was out of the way!

WHO ARE YOU KYDDING?

Name: THOMAS KYD
Born: c. 1558 **Died:** c. 1594
Greatest works: The Spanish Tragedy (the most popular play of the day)
Life and times: When Marlowe was killed, his friend, Thomas Kyd was also arrested. He was tortured, hideously and painfully, stretched out on the rack, to make him dish the dirt about Marlowe's beliefs. Kyd said nothing. He spent months in prison and was so badly treated that he died shortly after his release.

SEEING RED

Name: BEN JONSON
Born: 1573 **Died:** 6 August 1637
Greatest works: *Every Man Out of His Humour; Volpone; The Silent Women; The Alchemist; The Devil is an Ass*
Life and times: *Actor, poet, playwright and bricklayer's son, Ben Jonson's fiery temper frequently landed him in trouble, and in jail. In 1598, he killed fellow actor Gabriel Spencer in a duel. Jonson was only saved from the gallows by reciting a 'neck verse'. In those days, you were let off your first hanging offence if you could recite a verse from the Bible. Jonson was branded on his thumb instead and given a warning. He was Shakespeare's lifelong rival, friend and fan.*

Jonson is buried in Westminster Abbey in London. On his grave is inscribed the words:

'O Rare Ben Jonson'.

SAYINGS OF SHAKESPEARE NO.1 - ON ACTING AND THE STAGE

Shakespeare's plays are full of characters talking about acting, dressing up as other people, putting on plays, and generally talking about the world as a stage.

All the world's a stage,
And all the men and women merely players.
(Or, 'We're all just actors on the stage of life.')
AS YOU LIKE IT

Life's but a walking shadow, a poor player
That struts and frets his hour upon the stage,
And then is heard no more.
(Or, 'You're born, you do a bit of living, and before you know it, it's over.')
MACBETH

Our revels now are ended. These our actors,
As I foretold you, were all spirits, and
Are melted into air, into thin air:
And like the baseless fabric of this vision,
The cloud-capp'd towers, the gorgeous palaces,
The solemn temples, the great globe itself,
Yea, all which it inherit, shall dissolve,
And, like this insubstantial pageant faded,
Leave not a rack behind. We are such stuff
As dreams are made on, and our little life
Is rounded with a sleep.
(Or, 'Nothing is quite what it seems.')
THE TEMPEST

Get your apparel together, good strings to your beards,
new ribbons to your pumps...every man look over
his part...And, most dear actors, eat no onions, nor garlic,
for we are to utter sweet breath.
(Or, 'Prepare to meet your public.')
A MIDSUMMER NIGHT'S DREAM

BY ROYAL COMMAND

COURT APPEARANCES

In Shakespeare's day, the Queen or King didn't go to the theatre. The theatre came to them. The Lord Chamberlain's Men were regularly summoned to appear at Court, particularly at Christmas and New Year. In fact, Shakespeare wrote *The Merry Wives of Windsor* especially for the Queen because she liked the character of Falstaff so much. (Sir John Falstaff also appeared in *Henry IV, Parts 1 and 2.* He was louder and larger-than-life, and very fond of eating, drinking and making merry.) For Court performances, a temporary stage was set up inside the palace. Actors also performed for the law students at the Inns of Court in London. The first performance of *The Comedy of Errors* was given there in December 1594. Meanwhile, Shakespeare's fame spread far and wide. Plays, such as *Hamlet*, were performed by sailors on ships bound for the East Indies. It kept them out of mischief, the captain said.

DICING WITH DEATH

It wasn't easy being Queen. You tried being nice to people and all they did was turn against you. In 1601, Elizabeth's favourite earl, Essex, led a foolhardy rebellion to bring her down. (Shakespeare's patron, the Earl of Southampton was in on it too.) The rebellion failed and Essex was sent for the chop. The Lord Chamberlain's Men were lucky to escape a similar fate, as the night before the uprising, Essex had paid them to put on a special performance of *Richard II* at the Globe, in front of his supporters, complete with a scene where the king was deposed. This scene was usually left out of performances as the Queen didn't approve of it – for obvious reasons. When Elizabeth found out about this, she was livid! Meanwhile, the Lord Chamberlain's Men quaked in their boots. They were finally hauled before the government inquisitors but let off with a warning. The Queen had bigger fish to fry…

CURRICULUM VITAE

Name: Elizabeth Tudor (Elizabeth I)

Occupation: Queen of England

Born: 7 September 1533

Died: 24 March 1603

Star sign: Virgo

Parents: Henry VIII and Anne Boleyn

Reigned: 1558-1603

Marital status: Single (but flirted a lot). Said she was married to England!

Distinguishing features: Red hair (officially known as Royal Auburn). Elizabeth only allowed portraits to be painted which showed her at her best, with the famous Royal Auburn locks, ivory skin, ruby-red lips and gleaming white teeth. In fact, by the time of her death she was bald as a coot and had to wear a wig. She plastered her face with white powder and her teeth were yellow, rotting or missing altogether!

Hobbies and talents: Inherited the family trend for beheading people she didn't like (her father beheaded her mother!). Intelligent, shrewd, extremely good at ruling. Her reign was a golden age of exploration and literature.

ALL THE KING'S MEN

King James I loved the theatre, renaming Shakespeare's company the King's Men, and becoming their patron. The King's Men were great favourites at Court. The chief actors (Shakespeare included) were appointed 'Grooms of the King's Chamber'. Their pay (and work load) doubled. Between 1603-1613, they performed 177 times at Court. For James I's coronation (delayed because of plague), they were given four yards of scarlet cloth from the Royal Wardrobe for their uniforms.

REVELLING IN IT

The jolly-sounding Revels Office, headed by the Master of the Revels, was in charge of supervising Court performances. Each play was thoroughly censored and anything that might offend the Queen or King quickly rejected. Things looked black for playwrights whose work caused trouble. As a result of the *Richard II* fiasco, plays dealing with English history were banned for the time being.

CURRICULUM VITAE

Name: James Stuart (James I and James VI)
Occupation: King of England (and Scotland)
Born: 19 June 1566
Died: 27 March 1625
Star sign: Gemini
Reigned: 1603-1625
Parents: Mary, Queen of Scots and Lord Darnley
Marital status: Married to Anne of Denmark
Distinguishing features: Drooled as he ate. Very soft skin (he never washed his hands but only dabbed the ends of his fingers with a napkin). Weak legs. Broad Scots accent. Wore padded clothes in case of attack (Remember, remember the fifth of November?).
Hobbies and talents: Very extravagant. Easily bored (it's rumoured that Shakespeare kept Macbeth deliberately short - about two hours - because of the King's short attention span. Described as the 'wisest fool in Europe'. Intelligent and well-meaning but weak, stubborn and superstitious. (One of his favourite hobbies was witch-hunting - he was convinced that his rivals were hiring witches to assassinate him.)

THE COLLECTED WORKS

A POET IN THE MAKING

Although we know Shakespeare best for his plays, he was also a dab hand at poetry. Between 1592-94, while plague raged and the theatres were closed, Shakespeare penned two long poems, *Venus and Adonis*, and *The Rape of Lucrece*. Both were dedicated to his patron, the Earl of Southampton. Around that time, he also began a lot of shorter poems, the *Sonnets*, which he wrote off and on until 1600. A third long poem, *The Phoenix and the Turtle* followed about a year later. These poems were Shakespeare's first published works. People loved them!

WHO WAS THE DARK LADY?

Sonnets are poems consisting, usually, of 14 lines, though some of Shakespeare's have a few lines more or less. Shakespeare wrote 154 of them (over 2,000 lines in total). The later *Sonnets* are written to a beautiful woman, the mysterious 'Dark Lady'. But who was she? Was Shakespeare in love with her? And what did Anne Hathaway think of it all? All we know is that the Dark Lady had black hair, dark eyes, was good at music, and married! She might even have been a man!

Who knows?

THE PLAY'S THE THING...

Shakespeare wrote 37 plays, some long, some shorter, some better than others. Here's the complete list, in the order they were written. There are three categories –

tragedies (🎭) comedies (🎭) histories (👑)

SHAKESPEARE'S PLAYS

My top ten are marked with ★

1590	👑	Henry VI, Part 1
	👑	Henry VI, Part 2
	👑	Henry VI, Part 3
1592	👑	Richard III ★
	🎭	Titus Andronicus
1593	🎭	The Comedy of Errors
	🎭	The Taming of the Shrew
1594	🎭	The Two Gentlemen of Verona
	🎭	Love's Labours Lost
1595	🎭	Romeo and Juliet ★
	👑	Richard II
1596	🎭	A Midsummer Night's Dream ★
	👑	King John
1597	🎭	The Merchant of Venice ★
	👑	Henry IV, Part 1

1598	👑	Henry IV, Part 2
	🐵	The Merry Wives of Windsor
1599	👑	Henry V ★
	🐵	Much Ado About Nothing
	🦁	Julius Caesar
1600	🐵	As You Like It
	🐵	Twelfth Night ★
1601	🦁	Hamlet ★★★
1602	🐵	Troilus and Cressida
1603	🐵	All's Well That Ends Well
	🐵	Measure for Measure
1604	🦁	Othello ★
1605	🐵	Timon of Athens
1606	🦁	King Lear
	🦁	Macbeth ★
1607	🦁	Antony and Cleopatra
	🦁	Coriolanus
1608	🐵	Pericles
1609	🐵	Cymbeline
1610	🐵	The Winter's Tale
1611	🐵	The Tempest ★
1612	👑	Henry VIII (with John Fletcher)
	🐵	Two Noble Kinsmen (with John Fletcher)

IT'S A RECORD

LONGEST PLAY:
Hamlet
29,551 words in 4,042 lines

SHORTEST PLAY:
Comedy of Errors
1,778 lines, half the length of Hamlet

MOST DEMANDING PART:
Hamlet
The actor playing Hamlet has 11,610 words
and 1,569 lines to learn.

NUMBER OF SPEAKING PARTS:
1,277

MOST TWINS:
Comedy of Errors

Two sets – Antipholus of Ephesus and
Antipholus of Syracuse, and their servants,
Dromio of Ephesus and Dromio of Syracuse

MOST CASES OF MISTAKEN IDENTITY:

Comedy of Errors

See previous page. The two Antipholuses look identical but one is fiery, one is mild. The Dromios also look the same but one is stupid and one is bright. Confused? You will be!

LONGEST WORD IN SHAKESPEARE:

HONORIFICABILITUDINITATIBUS

Love's Labours Lost

GORIEST PLAY:

Titus Andronicus

Chiron and Demetrius, sons of Tamora, Queen of the Goths, are thoroughly nasty pieces of work. Titus Andronicus cuts their throats, then bakes them in a pie of blood and ground-up bones which he serves to their mother at a banquet!

Apart from this, there are ten or so other murders in the play, and plenty of chopping off limbs.

PLAY WITH MOST MISERY:

A matter of opinion, this, but the nominations are …

King Lear, *Macbeth* and … *Titus Andronicus!*

SHAKESPEARE'S SOURCES

So, where did Shakespeare get his information for all of those plays? How did he write about a Merchant of Venice if he'd never been to Italy? How much time did Shakespeare spend with his nose in other books? Or did he just make everything up?

Many of his ideas came from old, well-known, popular tales. He often pinched bits from here and there, reworking or adapting stories for his own purposes. For background reading, Shakespeare relied on his patrons' private libraries and on books and pamphlets bought from the bookstalls in the yard of St Paul's Cathedral. Here he could buy the latest travel books, legal and medical texts, folk-tales (which were *very* popular at the time), and translations from French, Italian and Latin.

For his history plays, Shakespeare's main source was *The Chronicles of England, Scotland, and Ireland*, published in 1577 by Raphael Holinshed and revised in 1586. Shakespeare sometimes altered ages and dates for dramatic effect.

For matters Italian, Shakespeare had a useful contact - an Italian friend, John Florio, who was tutor to the Earl of Southampton (Shakespeare's backer). If he was stuck for a name or wanted a fact checked, Florio was the man to call.

Write like Shakespeare

The Bible uses 8,000 different words. Shakespeare used 18,000. But he did make up about 1,700 of them or gave them different meanings. If you fancy writing a Shakespeare play, here are few of the Bard's own words to get you started:

Air-drawn	imaginary
Allycholly	melancholy, sad
Blunt-witted	dull, stupid
Bottom	a ball of thread (obviously!)
Burn daylight	to waste time
Buzzer	a tell-tale
By small and small	little by little
Canstick	candlestick (or a spelling mistake?)
Head-lugged	dragged by the head
Ich-eke	in addition
Sleeve-hand	wrist band
Sluggabed	someone who lies in bed for too long in the mornings (Sounds familiar?)
Sluggardise	to make lazy
Snapper-up	someone who snaps thing up
Snipe	a fool (also the name of one of the Bard's birds)
Snipt taffeta fellow	Someone who wanders around in slashed silk clothes. (Obviously more common then than now!)
Wistly	longingly
Wit-snapper	someone who tries to be witty, but fails!

Here's more information on my top ten plays.

No. 1
RICHARD III

DATE WRITTEN: 1592

SOURCES USED: Holinshed's *Chronicles* and *The Union of Two Noble and Illustre Famelies of Lancastre and Yorke* by Edward Halle

MAIN CHARACTERS:

RICHARD, DUKE OF GLOUCESTER *(RICHARD III)*

LADY ANNE *(HIS WIFE)*

DUKE OF BUCKINGHAM *(HELPS RICHARD TO THE THRONE)*

HENRY, EARL OF RICHMOND *(HENRY VII)*

THE PRINCES IN THE TOWER *(TWO)*

THE PLOT:

King Edward IV is dying. His evil (and ugly) brother, Richard, plots to seize the throne (despite being only fourth in line).

Various obstacles stand in his way. Richard has his brother, Clarence, sent to the Tower and killed (his body is hidden in a barrel of wine).

This niffs a bit!

Must have gone off.

He also sends his two nephews (one of them heir to the throne) to the Tower. Four other lords are killed. Richard is crowned king. The Princes in the Tower are killed. Finally, Richard himself is killed at the Battle of Bosworth Field, by Henry, Earl of Richmond, who becomes King Henry VII (Elizabeth I's grandfather). The night before the battle, Richard's evil past returns to haunt him as the ghosts of his victims appear at his bedside.

WHAT THEY SAID ABOUT RICHARD III:

This poisonous hunchback'd toad.

That bottled spider.

WHAT RICHARD III SAID OF HIMSELF:

Richard loves Richard.

I am determined to prove a villain.

FAMOUS LINES:

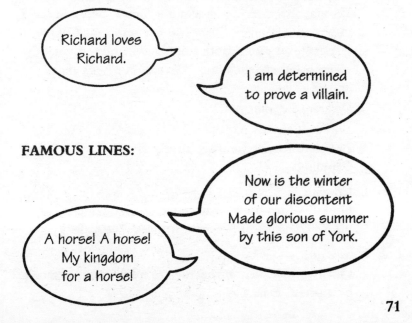

Now is the winter of our discontent Made glorious summer by this son of York.

A horse! A horse! My kingdom for a horse!

No. 2
ROMEO AND JULIET

DATE WRITTEN: 1595

SOURCES USED: *The Tragical Historye of Romeus and Juliet,* a poem by Arthur Brooke, published in 1562. (It was based in turn on a French translation of an Italian short story.)

MAIN CHARACTERS:

ROMEO MONTAGUE	JULIET CAPULET
THE MONTAGUES	THE CAPULETS
(AN ITALIAN FAMILY)	*(ANOTHER ITALIAN FAMILY;*
TYBALT *(JULIET'S COUSIN)*	*ENEMIES OF THE MONTAGUES)*
NURSE *(JULIET'S MAID)*	FRIAR LAWRENCE

THE PLOT:

1. Setting the scene

Verona, Italy. A long-standing feud between two important families, the Montagues and Capulets, reaches fever pitch. Both sides brawl, and throw taunts at each other, such as, '*Do you bite your thumb at us, sir?*'

2. A ball at the Capulets'

Enter Romeo Montague, in disguise. Across a crowded room, he falls madly in love with Juliet Capulet –

3. Later, that night...

Luckily for him, Juliet feels the same way – '*O Romeo, Romeo! Wherefore art thou Romeo?*'

4. Next day...

Our two love-struck sweethearts are married in secret by a priest, Friar Lawrence.

5. That afternoon ...

Tybalt (a Capulet) challenges Romeo to a duel. Romeo refuses. Tybalt kills Romeo's friend, Mercutio. Romeo kills Tybalt.

Take that!

Aaaghhh!

6. Romeo is banished by the Prince

7. Meanwhile ...

Juliet's parents have other plans for her – such as marrying Paris, a relation of the Prince.

8. Juliet has a cunning plan.

Juliet takes a sleeping potion and pretends to be dead, while Friar Lawrence goes in search of Romeo.

9. Things start to go wrong ...

Romeo hears that Juliet is dead. Unfortunately the letter Juliet has sent him to explain things doesn't arrive in time, and Romeo rushes back to Verona.

10. Romeo enters Juliet's tomb ...

He sees her lying there, thinks she's dead, drinks some poison and dies at her side ...'*Thus with a kiss I die.*'

11. Things go from bad to worse.

Juliet wakes up, sees Romeo, stabs herself and falls down dead (really dead, this time).

12. The whole story comes out.

The Montagues and Capulets make up, better late than never. Though too late for some, of course.

No. 3
A MIDSUMMER NIGHT'S DREAM

DATE WRITTEN: 1596

SOURCES USED: Too many to mention. including a collection of stories entitled *A Gorgeous Gallery of Gallant Invention*, published in 1578.

MAIN CHARACTERS:

THESEUS *(DUKE OF ATHENS)*
HERMIA *(IN LOVE WITH LYSANDER)*
LYSANDER *(IN LOVE WITH HERMIA)*
DEMETRIUS *(IN LOVE WITH HERMIA)*
HELENA *(IN LOVE WITH DEMETRIUS)*
OBERON *(FAIRY KING)*
TITANIA *(FAIRY QUEEN)*
PUCK *(A GOBLIN)*
BOTTOM *(A WEAVER)*

THE PLOT:

Hermia loves Lysander but is being forced to marry Demetrius. Hermia and Lysander run away together. Demetrius and Helena (also lovers) go too. They get as far as a wood near Athens which turns out to be full of fairies. Bewitched by Oberon, Titania, Queen of the Fairies, falls madly in love with the first man she sees – Bottom, the weaver, whose head has been magically transformed into that of a donkey! He and his friends are rehearsing a play in honour of Theseus's forthcoming marriage. (Okay, so it's a very popular wood!).

What lovely big ears you've got!

Oberon orders Puck to try out his magic love potion on the four young lovers but things go wrong and both Lysander and Demetrius fall in love with Helena. Oberon has had his fun and puts things right. Titania is released from her spell. A triple wedding is arranged for Hermia and Lysander, Demetrius and Helena, and the Duke and his bride. And everyone lives happily ever after.

DID YOU KNOW?

- In 1662, Samuel Pepys called *A Midsummer Night's Dream*, 'The most insipid, ridiculous play that ever I saw in my life'.

- In a 1911 production of the play, there was real grass, flowering shrubs, thickets of bluebells and rabbits running about the stage.

- The play may have been written to celebrate a court wedding, perhaps between William, Earl of Derby (Lord Strange's brother) and Lady Elizabeth Vere.

No. 4
THE MERCHANT OF VENICE

DATE WRITTEN: 1597
SOURCES USED: Two ancient folk stories,
   The Bond of Flesh and *The Casket Choice*.
MAIN CHARACTERS:

   SHYLOCK *(A RICH JEW AND MONEYLENDER)*
   PORTIA *(A RICH HEIRESS)*
   JESSICA *(SHYLOCK'S DAUGHTER)*
   ANTONIO *(A MERCHANT OF VENICE)*
   BASSANIO *(HIS FRIEND; PORTIA'S SUITOR)*
   LAUNCELOT GOBBO *(A CLOWN)*

THE PLOT:

Antonio borrows 3,000 ducats from Shylock to
help out a friend, Bassanio, who's in love with
Portia. If he can't pay it back by the date agreed,
he has to give Shylock a pound of his own flesh.
Meanwhile, Portia's suitors are
having a testing time. If they
choose the right casket
(from gold, silver and
lead), they get their girl. If
not, it's curtains for the lot
of them. Bassanio
strikes lucky (it's
the lead one) and
marries Portia.
Then they hear
the terrible
news...

Eeny,
meeny,
miny, mo...

Antonio can't pay back the money and Shylock wants blood (well, flesh). The claim goes to court. Portia, disguised as a lawyer, pleads for mercy on Antonio's behalf. Shylock refuses. Until, that is, Portia points out that Shylock is owed flesh, but not blood. If 'one jot of blood' is shed in the cutting of the pound of flesh, Shylock's for the high jump. Shylock relents. He is made to forfeit half his fortune to Antonio who gives it to Jessica, Shylock's daughter.

FAMOUS LINES:

> The quality of mercy is not strained.
> It droppeth as the gentle rain from heaven
> Upon the place beneath. It is twice blest.
> It blesseth him that gives, and him that takes.
> (PORTIA)

> If you prick us, do we not bleed? If you tickle us, do we not laugh? If you poison us, do we not die? And if you wrong us, shall we not revenge?
> (SHYLOCK)

UNSUNG HEROES NO. 1: OLD GOBBO

Old Gobbo, blind father of Launcelot Gobbo. Appears briefly in Act II Scene ii, with a dish of doves he's prepared for Shylock. Rather overshadowed by his son, who livens things up by acting the fool. Launcelot also takes messages between the main characters, always using twenty words where two would do.

No. 5
HENRY V

DATE WRITTEN: 1599
SOURCES USED: Holinshed's *Chronicles (Book III)*
MAIN CHARACTERS:

> HENRY V *(MODEL KING - BRAVE, DUTIFUL AND*
> *READY FOR ANYTHING)*
>
> GOWER *(ENGLISH CAPTAIN)*
> FLUELLEN *(WELSH CAPTAIN)*
> KING CHARLES VI OF FRANCE *(HALF-WIT)*
> KATHERINE *(FRENCH PRINCESS; HENRY'S WIFE TO BE)*

THE PLOT:

King Henry V is hopping mad. He's been sent a box of tennis balls by Prince Lewis of France, the Dauphin, to remind him of his misspent youth. At once he sets out to invade France and teach Prince Lewis a lesson. The army arrives in France and begins to march. Soon, they are wet, cold, tired and fed up. Henry musters all his kingly might to spur them on:

'*Once more unto the breach, dear friends, once more!*'

This does the trick. Heavily outnumbered, the English troops ('*We few, we happy few, we band of brothers*') go on to beat the French at the Battle of Agincourt.

CURRICULUM VITAE

NAME: HENRY V (HAL, TO HIS FRIENDS)

OCCUPATION: KING OF ENGLAND

BORN: 1387

DIED: 1422

CROWNED: 20 MARCH 1413, AGED 26

ROLE MODELS:

1) KING ARTHUR (OF ROUND TABLE FAME)

2) HONEY-BEES

'For so work the honey-bees,
Creatures that by a rule in nature teach
The act of order to a peopled kingdom.'

GREATEST MOMENT:

25 October 1415: The Battle of Agincourt, where Henry's army of 13,000 fought and defeated 50,000 French soldiers. A key point in the Hundred Years War (1337-1453) between England and France. By 1420, Henry had France at his feet. He'd married the French king's daughter and was named heir to the throne.

WORST MOMENT:

With all that going for him, he went and died!

No. 6
TWELFTH NIGHT
(OR WHAT YOU WILL)
(OR WHAT YOU, WILL?)

DATE WRITTEN: 1600

SOURCES USED: *Gl'Ingannati* (*The Deceived*), an Italian comedy acted in 1537; *A Farewell to the Military Profession*, a tale written by Barnaby Rich in 1581

MAIN CHARACTERS:

ORSINO *(DUKE OF ILLYRIA)*

VIOLA

SEBASTIAN *(HER LONG-LOST TWIN BROTHER)*

OLIVIA *(A RICH COUNTESS)*

SIR TOBY BELCH *(OLIVIA'S UNCLE)*

SIR ANDREW AGUECHEEK *(OLIVIA'S SUITOR)*

MALVOLIO *(OLIVIA'S POMPOUS SERVANT)*

FESTE *(OLIVIA'S FOOL)*

Now let me get this straight.

THE PLOT:

Duke Orsino is trying to woo Olivia, with the help of his page, Cesario (Viola in disguise). Olivia refuses Orsino but falls in love with Cesario (really Viola). To make matters worse, Viola (disguised as Cesario) falls in love with Orsino (as himself).

Meanwhile, Sir Toby Belch (the worse for drink), Sir Andrew Aguecheek and Feste convince snooty Malvolio that Olivia's in love with him. They fake a letter from Olivia telling Malvolio she'd fancy him rotten if only he'd wear yellow stockings, crossed garters and a smile – which he duly does. Instead, Olivia thinks Malvolio's gone mad and locks him up. (Besides, she hates the colour yellow.) Sebastian arrives in Illyria to find Viola. Olivia thinks he's Cesario (really Viola) and persuades him to marry her. Orsino sees through Cesario's disguise and marries Viola (really!).

FAMOUS LINES:

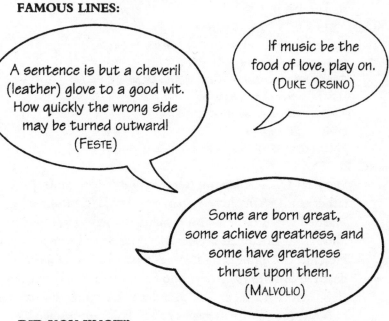

A sentence is but a cheveril (leather) glove to a good wit. How quickly the wrong side may be turned outward! (FESTE)

If music be the food of love, play on. (DUKE ORSINO)

Some are born great, some achieve greatness, and some have greatness thrust upon them. (MALVOLIO)

DID YOU KNOW?

● Illyria's not a real place. Shakespeare made it up.

● The first ever Feste was Robert Armin, a clown who joined the Lord Chamberlain's Men in 1599.

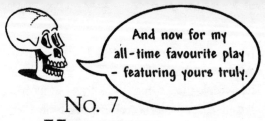

And now for my all-time favourite play – featuring yours truly.

No. 7

HAMLET

(OR THE TRAGEDY OF HAMLET, PRINCE OF DENMARK)
(OR WHAT DO YOU EXPECT FROM A MAN WHO TALKS TO SKULLS?)

DATE WRITTEN: 1601

SOURCES USED: An ancient story from the *Historica Danica* by the Danish writer, Saxo Grammaticus, and the *Histoires Tragiques*, retold by François de Belleforest in 1582.

MAIN CHARACTERS:

CLAUDIUS *(KING OF DENMARK; HAMLET'S UNCLE)*

HAMLET *(SON OF THE LATE KING)*

GERTRUDE *(HAMLET'S MOTHER; QUEEN OF DENMARK)*

HORATIO *(HAMLET'S FRIEND)*

OPHELIA *(HAMLET'S GIRLFRIEND)*

LAERTES *(HER BROTHER)*

POLONIUS *(HER FATHER, THE LORD CHAMBERLAIN)*

THE PLOT:

Hamlet's Uncle Claudius (secretly) murders Hamlet's father and (shamelessly) marries Hamlet's mother. Warned by his father's ghost, Hamlet vows to kill his murderous uncle. As cover, he pretends to be mad. He chucks Ophelia, then stages a play of his father's death in front of his uncle who has GUILTY written right across his face. Still Hamlet can't quite finish him off, though he manages to kill Polonius instead. Hamlet is rumbled. Now Claudius is out for his blood. Ophelia goes mad and drowns herself. In a fencing match (it's a set-up), Laertes stabs Hamlet with a poisoned foil. Hamlet kills Laertes. Gertrude dies from drinking poison (meant for Hamlet). Claudius dies. And, finally, Hamlet dies.

CURRICULUM VITAE

NAME: HAMLET

OCCUPATION: PRINCE OF DENMARK

EDUCATION: UNIVERSITY OF WITTENBERG

CHARACTER: *A sensitive soul but a bit of a ditherer. Thinks too much before he acts. Then talks himself out of doing anything. (Of course, if he had acted more quickly, the play would have ended three hours too early!)*

FAVOURITE COLOUR: BLACK

WORST MOMENT: *Mistaking the bumbling Polonius for a rat, and killing him.*

kill the murderer!

It's just not that simple dad!

FAMOUS LINES:

> To be, or not to be; that is the question:
> Whether tis nobler in the mind to suffer
> The slings and arrows of outrageous fortune,
> Or to take arms against a sea of troubles,
> And, by opposing, end them?

UNSUNG HEROES NO. 2: THE GRAVEDIGGERS

The gravediggers make a brief appearance in Act V scene i. They sing and tell jokes while digging Ophelia's grave. They also unearth Yorick's skull, just as Hamlet walks by:

> Alas, poor Yorick.
> I knew him, Horatio.
> A fellow of infinite jest, of
> most excellent fancy.

DID YOU KNOW?

- A full-length *Hamlet* takes five hours but is usually cut to four.

- Shakespeare may have played the ghost of Hamlet's father in the very first performance of the play. The ghost tells Hamlet of his uncle's wickedness.

- In 1787, *Hamlet* was performed without Hamlet, who was too nervous to appear. Many thought the play better off without him!

- One of the greatest Hamlets was the actress, Sarah Bernhardt. She played the part at the age of 55, with a wooden leg.

No. 8
OTHELLO

DATE WRITTEN: 1604

SOURCES USED: A French translation of an Italian tale, *Gli Hecatommithi* by Giraldi Cinthio (published in 1565)

MAIN CHARACTERS:

OTHELLO *(A NOBLE MOORISH GENERAL)*

DESDEMONA *(HIS LOVELY WIFE)*

IAGO *(OTHELLO'S RIGHT-HAND MAN)*

EMILIA *(HIS WIFE)*

CASSIO *(OTHELLO'S LIEUTENANT)*

BIANCA *(OTHELLO'S MISTRESS)*

THE PLOT:

The story so far. Venice. Othello secretly marries the lovely Desdemona. They are madly in love. He is black. She is white. Even then, this causes problems. War breaks out. They set off for Cyprus. Iago (the villain) starts to stir things. He tells Othello that Desdemona's having an affair with Cassio. Desdemona drops her hanky. Iago gets hold of it, plants it on Cassio, who gives it to Bianca. Othello sees her using the hanky for sewing practice. All hell breaks loose. He accuses Desdemona of giving the hanky to Cassio and thus being unfaithful. She denies it. He smothers her with a pillow and *Oh no I didn't!* immediately regrets it. Too late, he realises that the whole thing's Iago's lie. In his grief, he stabs himself, falls on the lovely (but dead) Desdemona's bed, and dies. *oh yes you did!*

THE MORAL OF THE STORY...

> O! beware, my lord,
> of jealousy:
> It is the green-eyed
> monster which doth mock
> The meat it feeds on.
> (Iago to Othello)

CURRICULUM VITAE

NAME: OTHELLO

OCCUPATION: MOOR OF VENICE; ARMY GENERAL

MARITAL STATUS: MARRIED (BRIEFLY) TO DESDEMONA

CHARACTER: *Noble and idealistic but prone to jealousy. Describes himself as 'one that loved not wisely but too well'.*

GREATEST MOMENT: *Marrying Desdemona, despite gossip.*

WORST MOMENT: *Catching Bianca with that handkerchief.*

UNSUNG HEROES NO. 3: THE HANDKERCHIEF

A non-speaking part, the hanky still steals the show. It's a gift from Othello (given to his mother by an Egyptian who said it had magical powers). (It may be magic but it's not even new!) Without the hanky, there'd be no evidence and no play. Emilia couldn't give it to Iago. He couldn't plant it on Cassio. He couldn't give it to Bianca for Othello to see. A definite case of hanky panky!

DID YOU KNOW?

During one performance of *Othello*, a member of the audience took out a gun and shot Iago. Another person, in another performance, threatened to wring Iago's neck. In the original Italian tale, Desdemona is killed by a falling bed!

MACBETH
(THE SCOTTISH PLAY)

DATE WRITTEN: 1606
SOURCES USED: Holinshed's *Chronicles*
MAIN CHARACTERS:

MACBETH *(SCOTTISH GENERAL)*
LADY MACBETH *(HIS WIFE)*
MACDUFF *(SCOTTISH NOBLEMAN)*
BANQUO *(SCOTTISH GENERAL)*
DUNCAN *(KING OF SCOTLAND)*
THREE WITCHES *(ASSORTED)*

THE PLOT:

On their way back from a victorious battle, Macbeth and Banquo stumble across three witches. They prophesy that Macbeth will be Thane of Cawdor, then King, and that Banquo's sons will also be kings. And lo and behold! No sooner does Macbeth reach home, than the King indeed makes him Thane. This isn't enough for Lady Macbeth. She goes on and on and on, until Macbeth gives in and murders the King. (Unfortunately for Duncan, he's staying at the Macbeths' at the time.) Macbeth is crowned King. He kills Banquo, just in case. Banquo's ghost haunts him while he's having dinner. He sets off to fight Macduff (the witches warned he's trouble). Lady Macbeth is tormented by guilt and kills herself. Macbeth is killed by Macduff. Malcolm (Duncan's son) is crowned king.

MEET THE MACBETHS:

MACBETH: Brave and sensitive but easily led. Under his wife's thumb. Macbeth is carried away by the glorious thought of being King, despite himself. But one murder leads to another, and soon he's in too deep to escape. Based on a real King Macbeth who ruled Scotland from 1040-1057.

LADY MACBETH: Ambitious and scheming. Very practical. She calmly tells her husband to wash the blood off his hands after he's murdered Duncan. Has a problem with sleepwalking. This is when her evil deeds come back to haunt her.

THE CURSE OF MACBETH:

Woe betide actors who say the 'M' word (i.e. Macbeth!). Bad luck is bound to follow. The play has been jinxed since the start. In the first-ever performance, the boy playing Lady Macbeth died backstage. A later performance went through four Macbeths in a week. Legs have been broken, dogs have died, scenery has fallen on actors' heads. Safer to say 'the Scottish Play' instead.

GETTING IT WRONG:

No. 10
THE TEMPEST

DATE WRITTEN: 1611

SOURCES USED: Accounts of the colonisation of America and of shipwrecks off the coast.

MAIN CHARACTERS:

PROSPERO *(A MAGICIAN AND THE RIGHTFUL DUKE OF MILAN)*

ANTONIO *(HIS BROTHER, WHO USURPED HIM)*

MIRANDA *(HIS DAUGHTER)*

CALIBAN *(HIS SLAVE)*

ARIEL *(A SPIRIT, FREED FROM A TREE)*

ALONSO *(KING OF NAPLES)*

SEBASTIAN *(HIS BROTHER)*

FERDINAND *(HIS SON)*

THE PLOT:

1. The story so far...

Having been set adrift by his wicked brother, Prospero and his daughter Miranda now live happily on an island.

2. A storm is brewing...

Prospero's enemies are sailing close by. He uses his magic powers to summon a tempest to shipwreck them.

3. The storm subsides...

Ferdinand is washed ashore. He sees Miranda. It's love at first sight!

4. Meanwhile, on another part of the island...

Antonio and Sebastian are plotting to kill Alonso while he sleeps. Ariel wakes him up with a song.

5. Somewhere else on the island...

Caliban, with Stephano and Trinculo, two drunken sailors, are plotting to murder Prospero.

6. Revenge is sweet...

Antonio and Sebastian get their come-uppance. Prospero invites them to a sumptuous meal which vanishes as soon as they tuck in. (A case of 'now you see it, now you don't!')

7. And gets sweeter...

Caliban and co. are chased round the island by spirit-dogs and soundly pinched.

8. The game's up!

Prospero lures the plotters into his cave and reveals his true identity.

9. Anything for a quiet life...

Prospero vows to give up magic. He sets Ariel and Caliban free (as long as Caliban mends his ways).

10. Time to go home...

Next day, they sail for Italy...

DID YOU KNOW?

- Caliban might be an (almost) anagram of 'cannibal'. Shakespeare had recently read an article about cannibals.

- Some people think Shakespeare modelled Prospero on himself. Prospero gives up magic just as Shakespeare is about to give up the theatre and return to Stratford.

- The action in *The Tempest* all takes place in a single day!

SHAKESPEARE'S BLOOMERS

Shakespeare sometimes altered the truth for dramatic effect. Sometimes, he simply got it wrong. Here's a selection of Shakespeare's best bloomers.

Well, nobody's perfect!

✘ In *The Winter's Tale*, a ship lands in Bohemia. Unfortunately, Bohemia is completely surrounded by land!

✘ A clock strikes in *Julius Caesar*, a play set in 45 BC. Clocks weren't actually invented for another thousand years.

✘ In *Antony and Cleopatra*, Cleopatra suggests playing billiards, a game not invented until about 1,500 years later.

✘ *King Lear* is set in Ancient Britain. Yet the Duke of Gloucester says he needs his 'spectacles' to read Edmund's letter. He was hundreds of years ahead of his time!

✘ *Titus Andronicus*, the ancient Roman general, occasionally lets slip the odd 'Bonjour' or 'Merci', despite the fact that that sort of French wasn't spoken yet.

Belch, Sir Toby	Olivia's drunken uncle in *Twelfth Night*
Bottom, Nick	Weaver in *A Midsummer Night's Dream*
Crab	A dog in *The Two Gentlemen of Verona*
Dowsabel	A name used to describe Adriana's buxom kitchen girl in *The Comedy of Errors*. She's got her eye on Dromio of Syracuse.

Dull, Anthony	A constable in *Love's Labours Lost*. He is Dull by name and dull by nature.
Dumb, Master	The name given to a waffling clergyman
Mouldy, Ralph	Recruited by Falstaff in *Henry IV, Part 2*
Mugs	A servant in *Henry IV, Part 1*
Oatcake, Hugh	A watchman in *Much Ado About Nothing*
Overdone, Mistress	A whore in *Measure for Measure*. She has had nine husbands.
Pompey, Bum	A clown in *Measure for Measure*
Shortcake, Alice	Slender's friend in *The Merry Wives of Windsor*. She borrows his Book of Riddles.
Simple, Peter	Slender's servant in *The Merry Wives of Windsor*
Sly, Christopher	A drunken tinker in *The Taming of the Shrew*
Sneak	Musician in *Henry IV, Part 2*
Snout, Tom	Tinker in *A Midsummer Night's Dream*
Sugarsop	A servant in *The Taming of the Shrew*
Thump, Peter	A servant in *Henry VI, Part 2*
Wart, Thomas	Recruited by Falstaff in *Henry IV, Part 2*
Whey-face	What Macbeth calls one of the servants

LOVE IN SHAKESPEARE'S PLAYS

Love figures large in Shakespeare's plays, though it doesn't always end well for those concerned. Here are a few of Shakespeare's most famous lovers and the sort of lovey-dovey things they said.

 1. Romeo Montague and Juliet Capulet

Play: *Romeo and Juliet*

Occupation: *'A pair of star-crossed lovers'*

Problem: Their families are bitter enemies.

Fate: Marry secretly against parents' wishes. Thinking Juliet is dead, Romeo drinks poison and dies. Juliet is not dead, sees Romeo's body, and kills herself.

Famous line:
'O Romeo, Romeo! Wherefore art thou Romeo?'

 2. Hermia; Helena; Lysander; Demetrius

Play: *A Midsummer Night's Dream*

Occupation: Four crazy, mixed-up kids.

Problem: Hermia loves Lysander and Helena loves Demetrius. Hermia is told to marry Demetrius. Both Lysander and Demetrius love Hermia. Later, they fall in love with Helena.

Fate: All's well that ends well. Hermia marries Lysander. Helena marries Demetrius.

Famous line:
'The course of true love never did run smooth!'

3. Antony and Cleopatra

Play: *Antony and Cleopatra*

Occupations: Roman general; Queen of Egypt

Problem: Antony loves Cleo and Cleo loves Antony. Ant hears that Cleo is dead and falls on his sword.

Fate: Cleo, who wasn't dead at all, clutches a poisonous snake to her bosom – on purpose. The snake bites her (poisonously) and she dies.

Famous line:
*'Age cannot wither her, nor custom stale
Her infinite variety.'*

SINGALONG-A-SHAKESPEARE

Songs from the shows

Some of the songs from Shakespeare's plays were big hits. Here's a selection of the catchiest ditties:

WHERE THE BEE SUCKS

Where the bee sucks, there suck I:
In a cowslip's bell I lie;
There I couch when owls do cry.
On a bat's back I do fly
After summer merrily.

(Chorus)
Merrily, merrily, shall I live now,
Under the blossom that hangs on the bough.
(ARIEL: *THE TEMPEST*)

IT WAS A LOVER AND HIS LASS

It was a lover, and his lass,
With a hey, and a ho, and a hey nonino,
That o'er the green corn-field did pass,
In the spring time, the only pretty ring time,
When birds do sing, hey ding, ding;
Sweet lovers love the spring.
(TWO PAGES: *AS YOU LIKE IT*)

FAIRIES' LULLABY

1 You spotted snakes, with double tongue,
Thorny hedge-hogs, be not seen;
Newts, and blind-worms, do no wrong;
Come not near our fairy queen.

(Chorus)
Philomel, with melody
Sing in our sweet lullaby;
Lulla, lulla, lullaby; lulla, lulla, lullaby:
Never harm,
Nor spell nor charm,
Come our lovely lady nigh;
So, good night, with lullaby.

2 Weaving spiders, come not here;
Hence, you long-legged spinners, hence;
Beetles black, approach not near;
Worm, nor snail, do no offence.

(Chorus)
Philomel, with melody, etc
(*A MIDSUMMER NIGHT'S DREAM*)

Dazzle your friends! Amaze your teachers! Surprise yourself by speaking Shakespeare the way the Bard did!

He that sleeps feels not the toothache.
(Or, 'Things always seem better in the morning.')
CYMBELINE

*They say best men are moulded out of faults
And, for the most part, become much better
For being a little bad.*
(Or, 'Nobody's perfect!')
MEASURE FOR MEASURE

*How sharper than a serpent's tooth it is
To have a thankless child!*
(Or, 'Kids!')
KING LEAR

Bid them wash their faces,
And keep their teeth clean.
(Or, 'Good Advice for Parents.')
CORIOLANUS

Some men are born great, some
achieve greatness, and some have greatness
thrust upon them.
(Or, 'There are many ways of making it.')
TWELFTH NIGHT

How far this little candle throws his beams!
So shines a good deed in a naughty world.
(Or, 'A little kindness goes a long way.')
MERCHANT OF VENICE

Delays have dangerous ends.
(Or, 'Whatever it is, do it NOW!')
HAMLET

Why then the world's mine oyster,
Which I with sword will open.
(Or, 'Go for it!')
MERRY WIVES OF WINDSOR

Brevity is the soul of wit.
(Or, 'The best jokes are short jokes!')
HAMLET

SHAKESPEARE RETIRES

Hi, honey! I'm home.

Do I know you?

QUITTING WHILE YOU'RE AHEAD

In 1612, Shakespeare put down his pen, packed his bags and headed home for Stratford. He still visited London now and again to catch up with friends and deal with his business interests. But he sold his shares in the rebuilt Globe and never wrote a play again. A lot of people wanted to know why. Had he run out of steam? Had he run out of ink? The answer was probably simpler than that. Shakespeare was quitting while he was ahead!

THE LAST PLAYS AND THE LOST PLAY

Shakespeare's last two plays, *Henry VIII* (1612) and *The Two Noble Kinsmen* (1613), were not all his own work.

His co-author was John Fletcher who took over from Shakespeare as the King's Men's main playwright. Another Shakespeare/Fletcher production, *Cardenio*, was acted in 1613. But all copies of the manuscript have been lost.

MR SHAKESPEARE, I PRESUME?

It was a wealthy, well-respected Shakespeare who returned to Stratford. In 1596, the family had been granted its own coat of arms - a gold shield with a shaken spear and the motto '*Non, sans Droit*' ('Not without right'). Plain William Shakespeare, actor, playwright, genius and glove-maker's son was now *Mr* William Shakespeare, Gentleman. In those days, these things really mattered!

NEW PLACE

Shakespeare had already found a place to retire in. This was New Place, the second finest house in Stratford. He bought the house in 1597, for the princely sum of £60, out of the (pretty substantial) proceeds of his shareholding and play-writing.

New Place had a chequered past. A previous owner murdered his daughter with some rat poison he'd hidden under the carpet. Another past owner poisoned his father.

It was also to have a chequered future. In 1756, the house was pulled down by its owner, the Reverend Gastrell. He was sick and tired of the tourists who flocked to see the mulberry tree in the garden (said to be planted by Shakespeare himself), and who pinched bits of the tree as souvenirs and carved their initials on the trunk!

FAMILY FORTUNES

So, what had happened to the Shakespeares while Will was away? Anne Hathaway stayed in Stratford where she missed all the fun but didn't seem to mind. Hamnet, their son, died in 1596. Shakespeare's father died in 1601, his youngest brother, Edmund (also an actor) in 1607 and his mother in 1608.

But not everything was gloom and doom. In 1607, Shakespeare's eldest daughter, Susanna, married John Hall, a respected local doctor. Shakespeare's first granddaughter, Elizabeth, was born a year later.

Thomas Quiney, Shakespeare's other son-in-law, was a different kettle of fish. You couldn't trust him an inch. Let alone wish him to marry your daughter. So, in 1616, when he married Judith Shakespeare, her father was not very pleased. Things began badly, and got worse. Within a month of their wedding, Thomas admitted to an affair (for which he was fined five shillings) and was later in trouble for selling rotten wine in his wine shop.

DID SHAKESPEARE LIKE GARDENING?

Quite possibly! He needed *something* to while away his twilight years, so why not spend it in the large garden at New Place? He may even have planted the famous mulberry tree with his own fair hands.

There were lots of gardening manuals around for him to dip into, with advice on 'the choice of seeds, apt times for sowing, setting, planting and watering', and on how to arrange 'dainty herbs, delectable flowers, pleasant fruits and fine roots' for best effect.

'Go, bind thou up yond dangling apricots...
You thus employed, I will go root away
The noisome weeds, which without profit suck
The soil's fertility from wholesome flowers.'

(Gardener to servants: *Richard II*)

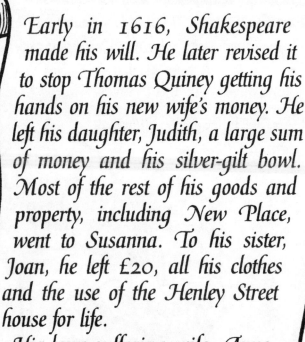

Early in 1616, Shakespeare made his will. He later revised it to stop Thomas Quiney getting his hands on his new wife's money. He left his daughter, Judith, a large sum of money and his silver-gilt bowl. Most of the rest of his goods and property, including New Place, went to Susanna. To his sister, Joan, he left £20, all his clothes and the use of the Henley Street house for life.

His long-suffering wife, Anne, gets just one mention:

'I give unto my wife the second best bed.'

But why? And just how many beds did Shakespeare have? It probably means that this was the bed Anne and William slept in, the first best bed being kept for guests. (Anne also received by right a third of his estate so she didn't do too badly.)

His London friends were not forgotten. Shakespeare left money (26s 8d) to three of the King's Men (Richard Burbage, John Heminges and Henry Condell) to buy memorial rings. These were worn in memory of dead friends or relations. He left similar amounts to friends in Stratford, including Hamnet Sadler.

Shakespeare's will survives to this day. Each of the three pages is signed, giving us half of the six famous signatures. And each of the pages is on a different-sized piece of paper.

The merry meeting

Shortly after signing his will, Shakespeare fell seriously ill with a fever. A few days before, he'd had a 'merry meeting' with his great friend, Ben Jonson and Michael Drayton, a poet. By all accounts, the wine flowed freely. And Jonson was famous for the amount he could drink. Perhaps the meeting was *too* merry for Shakespeare? Did the Swan of Avon die of drink? No one knows for sure.

There are several other theories. Did he die of shock brought on by Judith's marriage? Did his writer's cramp take a turn for the worse? Or was he murdered by Thomas Quiney, to get his own back? Whatever it was, it came on suddenly. For only a month before, he'd begun his will with a declaration of his '*perfect health and memorie*'.

THE WAY TO A DUSTY DEATH

Shakespeare died on 23 April 1616, his 52nd birthday. He was buried two days later in Holy Trinity Church, Stratford. According to a later report, they 'laid him full seventeen foot deep, deep enough to secure him'. The epitaph on Shakespeare's grave, penned by Shakespeare himself, reads:

> 'Good friend, for Jesus' sake forbear
> To dig the dust enclosed here;
> Blest be the man that spares these stones.
> And curst be he that moves my bones.'

Strong words indeed. Perhaps Shakespeare was afraid of his bones being dug up to clear space for another burial. It did happen. Space in the church was strictly limited. Or perhaps he took a long-held secret with him to his grave – the identity of the Dark Lady or the manuscript of his lost play, maybe. We will never know. The curse worked! No one has ever dared to disobey Shakespeare's last wish.

His family commissioned a bust in his honour. It was sculpted by Gerard Johnson, a stonemason who'd worked near the Globe in London. Shakespeare is shown with a quill pen in one hand and a sheet of paper in the other. One critic said it made him look like a 'self-satisfied pork butcher'!

> 'He was not of an age, but for all time!'
> BEN JONSON

'For mine own part I could be well content
To entertain the lag-end of my life
With quiet hours.'
(Or, 'Anything for a quiet life.')
HENRY IV, PART 1

'All that live must die,
Passing through nature to eternity.'
(Or, 'It comes to us all eventually.')
HAMLET

'Friends, Romans, countrymen, lend me your ears;
I come to bury Caesar, not to praise him.
The evil that men do lives after them,
The good is oft interred with their bones.'
(Or, 'Taking goodness to the grave.')
JULIUS CAESAR

SHAKESPEARE SINCE THEN

A NARROW SQUEAK

When the Globe burned down in 1613, an even greater disaster was narrowly averted. Some quick-thinking soul grabbed the play books just in time and rescued them from the flames. Otherwise, Shakespeare's plays would have been lost for all time. (Of course, you could argue that this would have saved a lot of trouble!)

The person who risked his neck to save Shakespeare's scripts was probably the actor, John Heminges. A ballad published the day after the fire describes him as appearing from the burning building, stuttering with shock and with 'swollen eyes' because of the smoke.

One day you'll thank me for this!

SHAKESPEARE IN PRINT

None of Shakespeare's plays appeared in print during his lifetime. At least, not officially. About half were published in cheap 'quarto' editions (about half the size of a magazine), costing sixpence each. Some of these are known as the 'Bad Quartos', as they were put together from notes secretly scribbled down during performances, from stolen prompt-books, or from bit-part actors paid to try to remember their lines. However, there's evidence that Shakespeare was definitely involved with the publication of some of them, or at least that the theatre was. These are known as the 'Good Quartos'.

THE FIRST FOLIO

In 1623, two of Shakespeare's fellow-actors, John Heminges and Henry Condell, gathered all the King's Men's scripts and play-books together and published the first official collection of Shakespeare's plays (36 in total). It was called the First Folio. All other editions followed its lead.

Over 200 of the original First Folios survive. (Which is just as well, as there is not a single copy of any of Shakespeare's original manuscripts.) In the introduction, Ben Jonson wrote a glowing tribute which began:

> *'Soul of the Age!*
> *The applause, delight, the wonder of our Stage!'*

This may have been written somewhat tongue in cheek. Jonson was great friends with Shakespeare but was sometimes irritated by all the attention he received.

Heminges and Condell added their own letter '*To the Great Variety of Readers*', in which they remarked that Shakespeare hardly ever made mistakes in his writing and rarely needed to cross things out. There is also a list of the principal actors in Shakespeare's plays, including the Bard himself, and an engraved portrait. To buy a copy cost 20 shillings (about three weeks' wages for an ordinary person).

A Second Folio was published in 1632, almost identical to the first. But a Third Folio, published in 1664, contained seven new plays, never seen before. Six of these weren't even by Shakespeare but nobody seemed to mind! (The other was *Pericles*, which was.)

REWRITING SHAKESPEARE

Two 18th-century writers, Nahum Tate and Colly Cibber, took it upon themselves to revamp some of Shakespeare's plays. The original versions were too depressing, they said. Tate gave *King Lear* a happy ending in which Cordelia married Edgar and lived happily ever after (in fact, she died). Cibber rewrote about half of *Richard III*, to make it more dramatic! These 'new' versions proved very popular with audiences and were the set texts used by actors for the next 150 years.

CATCHING THE BARD BUG

Within 60 years of his death, Shakespeare was in danger of being forgotten altogether. Not for long! A legend was soon in the making. Shakespeare-worshippers flocked to Stratford-upon-Avon (as they still do today) in search of their own little bit of the Bard. In no time at all there was a thriving market in fake souvenirs.

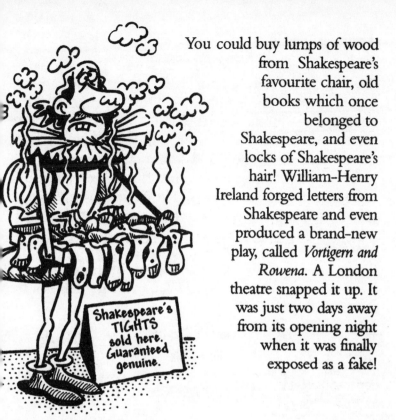

You could buy lumps of wood from Shakespeare's favourite chair, old books which once belonged to Shakespeare, and even locks of Shakespeare's hair! William-Henry Ireland forged letters from Shakespeare and even produced a brand-new play, called *Vortigern and Rowena*. A London theatre snapped it up. It was just two days away from its opening night when it was finally exposed as a fake!

SHAKESPEARE'S BIRTHPLACE

In 1847, Shakespeare's birthplace, the house in Henley Street, was put up for auction. The sale poster described it as *'The truly heart-stirring relic of a most glorious period, and of England's immortal bard...the most honoured monument of the greatest genius that ever lived'*. A bit of a mouthful but you got the message. The house was nearly bought by the circus-owner Phineas T. Barnum and shipped to America, piece by piece. It was saved in the nick of time and bought as a national monument to be preserved for ever. In its time, it had also been an inn, *The Swan and Maidenhead*, and a butcher's shop.

JUBILEE JAMBOREE

David Garrick (1717-1779) was the greatest Shakespearean actor of the 18th century. Shakespeare was his hero, and his hobby. In 1769, he organised the Shakespeare Jubilee celebrations in Stratford. The Jubilee was a disaster from beginning to end. It's true, there were fireworks, and cannons, *and* songs and speeches in Shakespeare's praise. But there was also a torrential downpour of rain. The River Avon burst its banks and almost swept the whole thing away.

SHAKESPEARE GETS EVERYWHERE

These are just a few of the thousands of things inspired by Shakespeare over the years. You name it, Shakespeare inspired it!

☛ **Musicals**
West Side Story
    (based on *Romeo and Juliet*)
Kiss Me Kate
    (based on
    The Taming of the Shrew)
The Boys from Syracuse
    (based on
    The Comedy of Errors)
Return to the Forbidden Planet
    (based on *The Tempest*)

☛ **Operas** 23 plays have been made into operas e.g.
Otello (Verdi)
A Midsummer Night's Dream (Britten)

☛ **Ballets** Including *Romeo and Juliet* (Prokofiev)

☛ **Symphonies and overtures**
Falstaff (Elgar)
Romeo and Juliet (Tchaikovsky)
A Midsummer Night's Dream (Mendelssohn).

☛ **Silent films** Including 17 versions of *Hamlet*

☛ **Films** Including a cartoon version of *Romeo and Juliet* called *Shakespearean Spinach*

☛ **Gardens** Planted with flowers, fruit and veg mentioned by Shakespeare

☛ **Tranquiliser drugs** For treating mental disorders such as those suffered by characters including Lady Macbeth and Ophelia

☛ **Golf courses** Yes, it's true! At Club Shakespeare, Atlanta, USA, the holes are named after Shakespeare plays.

And finally…

☛ **Bard-a-grams** – spouting love poetry for St Valentine's Day!

Who really wrote the plays?

Some people claim that Shakespeare couldn't possibly have written *all* those plays. How could a humble glovemaker's son, who'd never been to university and had never travelled abroad, pen such masterpieces? But if he didn't write them, then who did? Here are some of the main contenders:

1

Sir Francis Bacon (1561-1626)
Statesman, poet and philosopher

●◆ *Pros:* Legal background

Literary interests
Gardening interests
Royal connections (Lord Chancellor to James I)

●◆ *Cons:* With all this going for him, when did he find time to write 37 plays?

●◆ *Greatest fan:* Mrs Delia Bacon (no relation) of Ohio, USA (born 1811).

●◆ *Claim:* Supporters claim that Bacon hid a clue somewhere in the plays, for example, the word 'honorificabilitudinitatibus', an anagram of the Latin for 'Francis Bacon wrote these plays'. May have used Shakespeare's name as a pseudonym (pen-name).

●◆ *Verdict: A strong front-runner*

2

Edward De Vere (1550-1604)
17th Earl of Oxford

•◆ *Pros: Wrote plays in secret*
Royal connections
Lover of all things Italian

•◆ *Cons: Nasty nature (once skewered a cook*
with his sword)
Once farted in front of the Queen
Died before writing **King Lear, Macbeth,**
The Tempest *etc etc*

•◆ *Greatest fan: Thomas Looney, an English*
teacher. His problem was his name! One
publisher offered to publish his theory provided
he used a pseudonym. (He refused!)

•◆ *Claim: Supporters claimed that De Vere's*
interests and connections made him the
perfect Shakespeare

•◆ *Verdict: Fascinating but false*

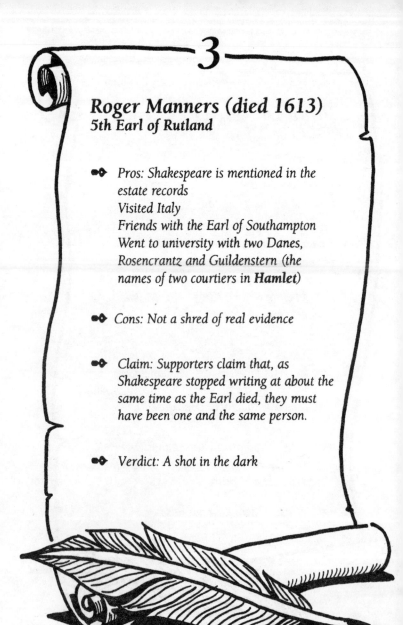

3

Roger Manners (died 1613)
5th Earl of Rutland

●◆ Pros: Shakespeare is mentioned in the
   estate records
   Visited Italy
   Friends with the Earl of Southampton
   Went to university with two Danes,
   Rosencrantz and Guildenstern (the
   names of two courtiers in **Hamlet**)

●◆ Cons: Not a shred of real evidence

●◆ Claim: Supporters claim that, as
   Shakespeare stopped writing at about the
   same time as the Earl died, they must
   have been one and the same person.

●◆ Verdict: A shot in the dark

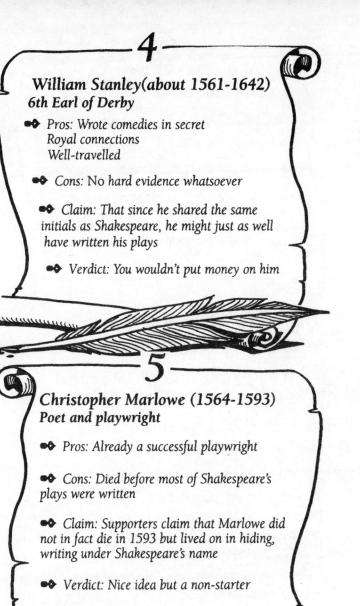

4

William Stanley (about 1561-1642)
6th Earl of Derby

•◆ *Pros: Wrote comedies in secret*
Royal connections
Well-travelled

•◆ *Cons: No hard evidence whatsoever*

•◆ *Claim: That since he shared the same initials as Shakespeare, he might just as well have written his plays*

•◆ *Verdict: You wouldn't put money on him*

5

Christopher Marlowe (1564-1593)
Poet and playwright

•◆ *Pros: Already a successful playwright*

•◆ *Cons: Died before most of Shakespeare's plays were written*

•◆ *Claim: Supporters claim that Marlowe did not in fact die in 1593 but lived on in hiding, writing under Shakespeare's name*

•◆ *Verdict: Nice idea but a non-starter*

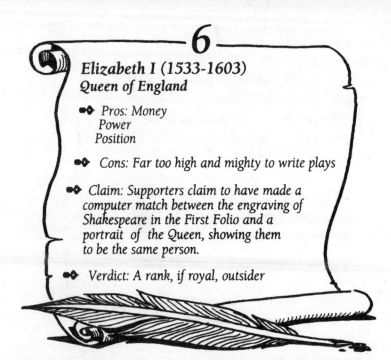

6

Elizabeth I (1533-1603)
Queen of England

- Pros: Money
  Power
  Position

- Cons: Far too high and mighty to write plays

- Claim: Supporters claim to have made a
  computer match between the engraving of
  Shakespeare in the First Folio and a
  portrait of the Queen, showing them
  to be the same person.

- Verdict: A rank, if royal, outsider

Of course Shakespeare wrote his own plays! The Royal Bacon Company simply doesn't sound right!

What they said about Shakespeare

The good and the not so good...

BEN JONSON, 1573-1637

> 'I remember the players have often mentioned it as an honour to Shakespeare that in his writing ... he never blotted out a line. My answer hath been, 'Would that he had blotted out a thousand.'

(Or 'Every line was one line too many, in my opinion!')

BEN JONSON, AGAIN, IN A BETTER MOOD

> 'There was ever more in him to be praised than to be pardoned.'

(Or 'But I suppose he wasn't all bad!')

THOMAS FULLER, 1608-1661

'Many were the wit-combats twixt him and Ben Jonson, which two I behold like a Spanish great galleon, and an English man-of-war; Master Jonson (like the former) was built far higher in learning; solid but slow in his performances. Shakespeare with the English man-of-war, lesser in bulk, but lighter in sailing, could turn with all tides, tack about and take advantage of all winds, by the quickness of his wit and invention.'

(Or 'They fought like cat and dog, but they liked each other really.')

SAMUEL TAYLOR COLERIDGE, 1772-1834

'I believe the souls of five hundred Sir Isaac Newtons would go to the making up of a Shakespeare...'

(Or 'Even the great Sir Isaac Newton, who discovered gravity, wasn't a patch on Shakespeare...')

GEORGE BERNARD SHAW, 1856-1950

'With the single exception of Homer, there is no eminent writer...whom I despise so entirely as I despise Shakespeare...It would positively be a relief to me to dig up his bones and throw stones at him.'

(Or 'Down with Shakespeare! I wish he were dead - except that he already is!')

ROBERT GRAVES, 1964

'The remarkable thing about Shakespeare is that he is really very good — in spite of all the people who say he is very good.'

(Or 'Shakespeare *was* all he was cracked up to be - it's official!')

119

DATES WITH SHAKESPEARE

1558	Elizabeth I is crowned Queen
1564	Christening of William Shakespeare (26 April)
	Birth of Christopher Marlowe
1568	John Shakespeare is elected Mayor of Stratford
1569	Visit of the Queen's Men to Stratford
1575/6	William attends Stratford Grammar School
1576	The Theatre is built in Shoreditch
1582	William Shakespeare marries Anne Hathaway (27 November)
1583	Susanna Shakespeare is christened (26 May)
1585	Christening of Hamnet and Judith Shakespeare (2 February)
1585/91	The Lost Years. Shakespeare seems to disappear.
1587	Philip Henslowe builds the Rose Theatre on Bankside
1588	The Spanish Armada is defeated
1590?	*Henry VI, Parts 1, 2 and 3* written
1592	Shakespeare is listed as an actor in the Lord Chamberlain's Men
	Death of Robert Greene (3 September)
	Philip Henslowe begins his diary
	First performance of Shakespeare's first play, *Henry VI Part 1*
	Richard III, Titus Andronicus written
1592/93	Plague hits London. The theatres are closed.
	Death of Christopher Marlowe (30 May)
	Shakespeare writes *Venus and Adonis* and *The Rape of Lucrece*
1593	*The Comedy of Errors* written
	The Taming of the Shrew written
1593/1600	Shakespeare writes the *Sonnets*

1594	Death of Ferdinando, Lord Strange (16 April)
	The Two Gentlemen of Verona written
	Love's Labour's Lost written
1595	*Romeo and Juliet* written
	Richard II
1596	Death of Hamnet Shakespeare
	The Swan Theatre opens
	A Midsummer Night's Dream written
	King John written
1597	Shakespeare buys New Place, Stratford
	The Merchant of Venice written
	Henry IV, Part 1 written
1598	*Henry IV, Part 2* written
	The Merry Wives of Windsor written
1599	The Globe Theatre is built
	Henry V written
	Much Ado About Nothing written
	Julius Caesar written
1600	The Fortune Theatre opens
	As You Like It written
	Twelfth Night written
1601	The Earl of Essex is beheaded after a failed plot against the Queen
	Death of John Shakespeare
	Hamlet written
1602	*Troilus and Cressida* written
1603	Death of Elizabeth I (24 March)
	Plague closes the theatres
	James I is crowned king (25 July)
	Shakespeare's company becomes the King's Men by Royal Appointment
	All's Well That Ends Well written
	Measure for Measure written
1604	*Othello* written

1605	The Gunpowder Plot (5 November)
	Timon of Athens written
1606	*King Lear* written
	Macbeth written
1607	Susanna Shakespeare marries Dr John Hall (5 June)
	Coriolanus written
	Antony and Cleopatra written
1608	Death of Mary Shakespeare
	Pericles written
1609	The King's Men take over the Blackfriars Theatre
	Plague closes the theatres
	Cymbeline written
1610	*The Winter's Tale* written
1611	*The Tempest* written
1612	*Henry VIII* written
	Shakespeare retires to Stratford
1613	*Two Noble Kinsmen* written
	The Globe Theatre burns down (29 June)
1614	The Globe is rebuilt and back in business
	The Hope Theatre opens
1616	Shakespeare drafts his will
	Judith Shakespeare marries Thomas Quiney
	Death of William Shakespeare (23 April)
1619	Death of Richard Burbage (13 March)
1623	Death of Anne Hathaway
	The First Folio is published
1625	Death of James I
1642	The theatres are closed by order of Parliament

BEAT THE BARD

Now that you've finished this book, why not test your knowledge of Shakespeare in this brilliant quiz?

1) What else is celebrated on Shakespeare's birthday?
- a) Ben Jonson's birthday
- b) King James I's birthday
- c) St George's Day

2) What was Shakespeare's father?
- a) an actor
- b) a glove-maker
- c) a schoolmaster

3) Who did Shakespeare marry?
- a) Anne Whateley
- b) Agnes Smith
- c) Anne Hathaway

4) Where was the Globe built?
- a) Bankside
- b) Shoreditch
- c) St Paul's

5) What was a wherry?
- a) a ruff
- b) a weapon
- c) a ferry

6) What time did plays begin?
- a) 3 p.m.
- b) 2 p.m.
- c) 7.30 p.m.

7) Why did boys play the part of girls?
- a) they were better at it
- b) girls weren't allowed to act
- c) they were more boys than girls

123

8) What was a sharer?
 a) a part-owner of a theatre
 b) a ticket-seller
 c) a part-owner of a bear

9) Who was the Earl of Southampton?
 a) Queen Elizabeth's favourite
 b) an Elizabethan explorer
 c) Shakespeare's patron

10) How did Christopher Marlowe die?
 a) in prison
 b) in a tavern brawl
 c) of stage fright

11) What was a groundling?
 a) something you planted in the garden
 b) an apprentice actor
 c) someone who stood in the yard to watch a play

12) Who was the 'Dark Lady'?
 a) Anne Hathaway
 b) Queen Elizabeth I
 c) your guess is as good as mine!

13) Which is Shakespeare's longest play?
 a) *Hamlet*
 b) *Titus Andronicus*
 c) *Henry VI, Part 3*

14) Which of Portia's caskets is the right one?
 a) lead
 b) silver
 c) gold

15) What does the Dauphin of France send Henry V?
 a) French cheese
 b) tennis balls
 c) aftershave

16) Who was Hamlet's girlfriend?
 a) Jessica
 b) Miranda
 c) Ophelia

17) How did Desdemona die?
- a) a bed fell on her head
- b) Othello smothered her
- c) Othello shot her

18) Whose ghost spoils Macbeth's supper?
- a) Macduff's
- b) Hamlet's father's
- c) Banquo's

19) What is a sluggabed?
- a) a place where slugs sleep
- b) someone who stays in bed too long
- c) someone who hits people with beds

(see Question 17)

20) What did Shakespeare leave to Anne Hathaway in his will?
- a) his second best bed
- b) his first best bed
- c) his pen and pencil set

So how did you do?

ANSWERS:

1) c, see page 10
2) b, pages 16 and 14
3) c, page 24
4) a, page 41
5) c, page 31
6) b, page 37

7) b, page 47
8) a, page 54
9) c, page 56
10) b, page 57
11) c, page 37
12) c, page 63
13) a, page 66

14) a, page 76
15) b, page 78
16) c, page 82
17) b, page 85
18) c, page 87
19) b, page 69
20) a, page 10...

INDEX

READ ON

These are just a few of the hundreds of books on Shakespeare.
See what your local library or bookshop has in stock:

EXTRAORDINARY LIVES: SHAKESPEARE by Peter Hicks
(Wayland, 2013)
A biography of Shakespeare illustrated with photographs
and paintings of significant people and places.

SHORT, SHARP SHAKESPEARE by Anna Claybourne
(Wayland, 2014)
Fantastic retellings of some of Shakespeare's best-loved plays.
The plot of each play is transformed into a story, told in prose,
with lively, humorous illustrations from Tom Morgan-Jones.

THE COMPLETE WORKS OF SHAKESPEARE (any edition)
Shakespeare in his own words.

TRUTH OR BUSTED: SHAKESPEARE by Kay Barnham
(Wayland, 2014)
Humorously explores popular myths and legends to see
whether they are true or false.

WELL WORTH A VISIT

STRATFORD-UPON-AVON
Much changed since Shakespeare's day but you can still visit
Shakespeare's birthplace in Henley Street, New Place and
Anne Hathaway's cottage.

THEATRES
The RSC (Royal Shakespeare Company) has theatres in
Stratford-upon-Avon, and in London at the Barbican and at
The Globe Theatre, Bankside, (rebuilt just as it was in
Shakespeare's day).